AWKWARD IS THE NEW BRAVE

WIPEOUTS HAPPEN, GET BACK UP ANYWAY

BELLE LOCKERBY

A catalogue record for this book is available from the National Library of Australia

CONTENTS

For my kids,

Always be brave enough to be who you are, awkward enough to try out things that are hard, new and uncomfortable, and kind enough to be the safe space for those doing the same. I love you both – if the "grandma" police weren't around, I love yous.

Mum x

ACKNOWLEDGMENTS

It would be un-Australian of me not to thank the pubs and coffee shops that have kept me fed, caffeinated and connected to the internet over the past year, so I may as well start with you guys, as you have been my regular hangs while I have juggled meetings, mum life and the writing and re-writing of this book. Gordon St Garage, Moore & Moore, Blasta Brewing and Shorehouse – thanks for the food, coffee, courtesy and, mostly, your wi-fi. Deb and Mark of Jamaica Blue – it really has meant a lot having you ask how I'm progressing every day and keeping me on track. Thank you, I appreciate you – it's nice to be treated like family.

To my book team: Linda, the first conversations about writing a book – any book – started four years ago. Things got shelved, raised, shelved, and then actually happened. Your faith and confidence is nothing short of amazing, and I am so grateful for your support through this process. Thank you. Having someone believe in you is incredibly powerful. I'm so lucky that you have done that for me.

Kelsey ed: Thank you for allowing a first-timer to develop. I have learned so, so much through this process.

To the mums of Mandurah: What can I say? You are a force. Outside of my kids, there is nothing I am more privileged to be a part of. The community that has blossomed and thrived, it's a thing of beauty. You are all amazing lights. Be brave. Grow at your pace, within your means. Take the small wins – and the big wins. There are so many of you that I have been fortunate enough to get to know more over the years. Too many to list.

Chappy: Thanks for being a good co-parent. I think we are doing alright. I'm glad we are friends. I'm glad we are still family. I'm glad that we both wish happiness for each other.

The special ones who hold truth, adventure, laughter, safety and kindness in the same regard, and have been there for me when it's been dark, and when it's been light: Jo, Jaq, Jamie, Tarzy, Hayles, DiAnne, Minds, ToTo. I love you, I appreciate you.

INTRODUCTION

Confession: I'm about 87 percent vegan.

Let me explain. I love kale and vegies and like to think that if there were an apocalypse (zombie or otherwise) I would eat pretty much a vegan diet except for the odd small animal I might catch and cook. I mean, I wouldn't stop to milk a cow – that would be too tricky, unless the zombies happen to be slow-moving zombies.

But… if I crossed a camp and someone had bacon on the go, I wouldn't say no. So, for the sake of simplicity, I tell people I'm 87 percent vegan.

What has this got to do with the book?

Well, while it is a memoir, and while this is my truth and my experience, I have had to use my 87 percent vegan rule for the sake of simplicity and protection. Not from zombies, but from being sued. I'd rather not be sued. It's not on my bucket list. Streaking as an 82-year-old lady: yes. Being sued: no.

So, in the interest of self-preservation and the preservation of loved ones, timelines have been skewed, names have been changed and a few real-life people have been merged into one character. Bit like something you would see happen to superheroes – which the people in my life are. It's about identity protection, unless they have said otherwise.

So yes, I was sent to live in a caravan park by my mum at 16, yes all the people died, and yes I did all the things. But yes, I have had to protect the innocent, and sometimes the not-so-innocent, which was very hard for me to do, as I hold the truth in high regard. I hold the people I love in high regard, too.

Speaking of the people I love... Whether you are in here or not in here has nothing to do with how much I love you.

I love all of you – as you are, as you were, and as you will be.

If this book helps one person to embrace that awkward feeling which comes with being brave and helps one person live a little more, then I'm a happy woman.

I hope you will be brave. Even if for you that means just making it to tomorrow.

Because your life is a gift, and you are needed.

Yours in awkwardness and with much love.

PROLOGUE

"*N*o, Sissy, you can't jump in."

"Why?! You go in without floaties! I go in without floaties. Me can do it!"

"No, you can't!"

She was indignant. Standing there on the shallow steps of our fibreglass swimming pool. The handmade leopard print bikini tied above her chubby toddler thighs. Yellow Floaties hugging chubby little arms. Blonde, bobbed hair over big, blue eyes with a smattering of freckles. Beautiful. Unlike yours truly with a pixie-cut fringe and long, scraggly sides – boy-type hair courtesy of self-administering a haircut ('cause that's what you did when you started school). An ugly duckling, as my mum had said. Ducks could swim, though. Quite well for five.

The yellow Floaties were ceremoniously ripped off from her arms.

"Sissy! Don't do it – you can't swim."

"Yes, me can!"

I watched her step down into the white fibreglass pool. The texture was

1

rough. Like sand and concrete mixed together. My kneecaps had been scarred by its roughness into circles from constant scraping.

Mum was inside. Somewhere.

It only takes a split second, really. It happened fast, and in slow motion.

Down she went. To the bottom. A metre from the safety of the steps. It doesn't take much for a kid to start to drown.

I dropped to the ground, lying on my stomach, the cement warm from the heat and the water, reaching in to hoist her up by her leopard print string bikini. Not the easiest thing, as it started to loosen.

I twisted my arm to make it tight.

Panicked!

"MUM! MUM! MUUUUUUUUUM! Sissy's drowning!"

I watched Sissy's face look at me, struggling to keep those blue eyes and smattering of freckles above the waterline.

Mum looked up from the kitchen window and stared.

"MUM! HURRY UP!"

And so I saved her. I thought I was being brave.

SOMETIME IN 1984

"You need to tell her!"

I cowered on the floor, looking at the tiny brown square tiles. Desperately trying to hide my body. Shame. Secrecy. Immense shame over my body. I was the protector. I would not fail in my duty.

"HAS SOMETHING HAPPENED?" My mum's voice interrogated me.

I tried to make like a slater bug and curl up, becoming a vault.

"Nothing, Mum! There's nothing!" I willed my eyes not to well with tears. Stubbornness. Determination, maybe.

"You need to tell her," Sissy pleaded.

"THERE IS NOTHING TO TELL!"

I tried to cover myself and shut the whole thing down.

She didn't know why my behaviour had changed. She was trying to figure it out.

I remained tight-lipped. I mean, how could I say anything? If I did, he would hurt her. He'd said so. If I said a peep, someone might hurt him, too, and it would be all my fault.

So I chose secrecy.
I chose a happy, fake front. 'The Protector'. My choosing.
I chose to keep it hidden.
I chose to keep me hidden.
And so I saved her. I thought I was being brave.

1

JANUARY, 2018

So here I am. About to get bitch-slapped by the green lady herself. A wake-up call.

The car park is full. An easterly is blowing. It's early morning, and the surf is filled with men – a bit like Collins Street in Melbourne during peak hour, except these guys are in wetsuits, not business suits. Their pace of life is different. They don't seem stressed. Maybe Becs is right. Maybe I can hand some stuff over to the ocean.

I grab my black-and-yellow boogie board and catch my reflection in a car window. The blue rashie is a bit tighter than it should be. The body is 20 kilos over where I'd like it to be. My eyes are puffy from the ugly crying about 20 minutes earlier on the phone to Becs.

I walk down the beach to where there are fewer people, dumping my physical stuff first. I haven't even swum out in the ocean since my triathlon days. The pre-kid days. The days where a different me existed. The days where I wasn't so concerned with sitting on the beach watching over the kids like a seagull watches over a hot chip about to be dropped, listening to the constant "Muuum! Muuum! Muuum! Muuuuum!" Sometimes they sound like the seagulls – sometimes I feel like the stray hot chip.

Looking out, I think about being here with zero kids in tow. It's their dad's turn this weekend. I have spent so much time sitting on the sand, watching my kids over the past five years that I forgot to participate.

Racing in takes courage. The contrast between the morning heat of summer and the coolness of the ocean shocks me again. A little like Becs' directive this morning. It was more like workout Becs than spiritual guru Becs.

Dutifully, I dunk my head in the water, willing the ocean to rush through my head and clean out everything I'm looking at for the next few months. I want to see how long I can stay under, like when I was a kid. I blow bubbles out until there is no air left in my lungs, listening to the swirling rush of the water, slightly losing my bearings while I am under the waves.

My thoughts swirl, too. A complete whitewash of overwhelm that if I'm not careful in choosing my thoughts will suck me down into the undertow. Work, missing family. Death anniversaries, in particular. Anniversary of Mum's death – 25 years approaching January 12. Anniversary of my older sister Wanita's death, 10 years in February. Her birthday in March. I outlive Wanita – 'Witchy' to me – this year. I'll turn 44. Any time I think of Witchy, though, I think of my duty to live fully. She never saw the snow – one of her dreams. I can't just live to work and give up on joy. I think of how she would be telling me that I'm not our mum. I won't turn into her.

Underneath the surface, no one can see me or hear me sobbing like some sad, depressed, brunette, frumpy, middle-aged version of the Little Mermaid. I can't stay under any longer, so I resurface.

"Huuumph." That's about the sound I make.

I stare out at the horizon, not thinking about sharks or anything, just thinking about how big the ocean is.

The ocean. Where my good friend Becs ordered me to go. The ocean that, right now, seems dead set on throwing me around like the leftover baked potato that my young son once threw at me across the dinner table in defiance.

I think the green lady is trying to whack some sense into me, perhaps. Either that or I am being given a bit of a, "Hey, screw you, human, I don't need your snot and tears – I'm salty enough. *You* can make a choice. *I'm* governed by the moon, and subject to how your race treats me."

Yet here I am. Waist-deep in a five-year-old, slightly sagging, mismatched bikini. One black-with-a-hibiscus-flower bottom piece, not really gripping like it should. One once-bright, fun fluoro-yellow top that is now faded, and jaded. All hidden under a stretched-a-bit-too-tight blue rashie over the muffin top. The loathed body space. Ugh. Another thing on the list. Dumb list.

The ocean doesn't really seem to care for the fact that I am ugly crying.

And when I say ugly crying, I mean *ugly crying*.

The only way I can differentiate from the sources of salt on my face is from touch. My tears are mixed with the ocean. But that slime to the left of my face – what the heck is that?

Oh, snot. Gross. I hate snot. More than vomit. More than baby nappies. It's just gross. Ew.

Yet, I am being obedient. Doing as my friend instructed.

I pause and duck under the ocean again, avoiding an angry wave, Becs' words echoing in my ears. "Stay there and hand it all over until you feel you can get out. Don't drown. Just hand all of it over to something bigger and more powerful than you. You will feel better. Go and do it now."

"Huuumph." Back under I go. This time, I scream back at the ocean when I let the air out, eyes closed tight. Kind of a primal scream. A scream trying to unleash whatever it was that was sitting there, blocking me. Fears. Fears of being sad. Fears of failing, despite succeeding in lots of areas. Fears of being fake.

More snot. And a giant chunk of seaweed.

I swipe my face, moving my hair, seaweed and snot out the way, and stare out at the vast green horizon in front of me. The big, slow-moving, shape-shifting waves that gather speed and force as they reach me in the water.

I turn back to the shore where I have left my black-and-yellow boogie board.

"How long, Becs? How long?"

I see her in my mind – short, choppy blonde bob. Tanned. Blue eyes. Then I hear her. "As long as it takes, chick, as long as it takes."

I actually hadn't heard her be that before – like she was on FaceTime earlier. Bossy and direct. I mean, well, except in the gym. Becs is not only a PT, but also an empath – quite in tune with all the woo in the world.

I stand there, bracing for the next wave, reflecting. I woke up this morning to one of my fears.

There are a few, it seems. Death by a hundred apartment cats as an old spinster lady. Frogs. Dying with regret. Going broke and having to go back to a 'real job'. Accidentally farting on an acupuncture table in front of the love child of Chris Hemsworth and Bradley Cooper – rock god crush Baker. Getting back out to date after two and a half years. Fuck, I think I'm neurotic. Maybe self-aware. Who knows.

The big fear, though? Today's front and centre, "Hey, how's your fucking life going?"

Sadness.

Truth be told, I am shit fucking scared of being sad.

I have started to fear feeling sadness and, well, quite possibly, feeling all the feels. I fear I will turn into my mum. She was dead at 49 (only five years away in my timeline) – something I desperately don't want for my two kids.

Another wave comes, and I think of how I woke up this morning under the overwhelming weight of responsibility. It was like my soul was the odd sock buried under the pile of laundry that is my life. I start replaying it with each wave that rolls through.

I was worried.

I was worried that I'd worked so hard to be strong and resilient through all the shit – abuse, death of family members, divorce… I worried that I was at risk of never being soft again. That I'd built walls so big, so strong, that trying to scale and get over those fuckers would be like trying to surf a barrel on a boogie board.

I was thankful my kids weren't home today to be watching me have a mid-summer meltdown.

I'd installed air conditioning at home that added to the feeling of fucking up. I regretted dropping $10K on it – I should know better than to hit cashflow that hard. But aside from that, life was, for all intents, really good. I had a house, two healthy kids, and co-parenting post-split was pretty good. I had a business I loved that was going well (yet I was scared that no one would come do the Mumpreneur programs this year, and then I'd be broke. With air conditioning. Selling the house in a bid to escape suburbgatory.)

I couldn't figure out why I had moved into this funk. It's not like I hadn't dealt with this time of the year before. For no logical reason, this morning I sat there with my phone and ugly cried.

To find normal, happy-go-lucky me caught in the dark undertow of sadness scared me.

To find normal, happy-go-lucky me in a downward spiral crying in bed, in particular, alarmed me even more. I was having a flashback. I was super-scared that the path I had tried so hard to avoid was now the karmic path I was going to find myself on anyway. A quick maths calc in my head and I figure I'm close to the age my mum was when I really saw her big, deep depression funk when I was 11 – close to my daughter Abby's age now.

I was having a flashback to 11-year-old me, and she was reminding me of why exactly I was scared. Of why I was worried. I feared sadness because I feared turning into Mum. And the age of my kids, especially my daughter, was paralleling this.

The happy but silenced little girl. The protector. The parent before her time. She was finding her voice. The little girl who wanted to learn to surf but had zero money. The girl who believed in God and knew of miracles. The girl who wants to remind the grown-arse woman that this, this space, this being in bed on a beautiful day... this is dangerous territory. So she takes me back.

Hey, do you remember? Remember how she was still in bed, and it was after three in the afternoon? On a school day?

Do you remember that something wasn't right? Remember how the room was dark? The curtains were drawn, even though the sun was out?

Remember how it wasn't the first day, either? It wasn't even the first week. You need to catch this now.

Remember how you didn't know what was wrong? Remember how sadness hung itself in the room along with despair?

Remember how the room smelled of sadness – if sadness were to have a smell?

It was Queensland in 1986. The 10-dollar note was crumpled in my small hand, next to the shopping list. The wooden floors creaked underfoot in the old shoddy Queenslander. I tiptoed, trying to be careful of where I stepped, not wanting to make too much noise.

It certainly looked like sadness. The curtains were drawn. Light tried to crack through as she lay there in the crumpled bed.

I think she had been there for three weeks, now, in the crumpled bed. Sadness had seeped in, and no happy lulls of my voice desperately trying to cheer her up and bring some alternate light into the room would change it.

Sadness smelled distressed. Like that musty old paper smell that the 10-dollar note had.

I watched the tears of my younger sister, Sissy, fall on her lifeless hands, even though she was not dead.

Nothing would stir her from the dark pit she had slid into.

Hope was missing. Maybe I could pass mine along. Maybe I could crack a joke and elicit a smile. That hope – it went missing in her. I don't even know why or how. I don't think she knew, either.

I didn't really know what was going on. I didn't have the words; I didn't have the knowledge. I doubt in 1986 many adults, let alone kids, had the language to describe depression.

I only knew what I had to do. Be quiet. Take the shopping list and 10 dollars. Walk the 20 minutes to the shop. Buy the ingredients. Come home. Cook Egyptian chicken for dinner for my sister and I. Get myself to bed. No hugs. No stories. Take my little bit of hope off to bed.

Hope that maybe, just maybe, in the morning she would get up, open the curtains and the light would come back in to counteract the dark that had seeped in everywhere.

She was motionless. Just staring blankly. I don't think even she knew how she had slid into the hole. I don't think she was aware of the smell in the room. That happiness was not in there – not in any form.

The smell would change later in the day, though, as I worked through the shopping list passed over in the dark.

I'd walk down the creaky steps of the Queenslander, embrace the heaviness of the tropical air and the sun, hotfoot it down to the shops where the air conditioning vents would blow some relief and joy in my direction, at least for a minute.

Buy chicken, and traipse back up, being careful not to disturb her too much as she stayed trapped in an open room.

The chicken – ew – gosh it was slimy.

I'd sprinkle Egyptian seasoning over the chicken. Cut lemons and put them inside. Turn the black, plastic knob to about 7 o'clock and carefully light the gas pilot light in the crappy old oven.

Mum's voice echoed in my memory: "Careful, we don't want the smell of burning hair and another pixie-cut fringe again, do we?" No, I didn't. It was bad enough being called a boy by an old lady in the playground the first time when I was six. This 1980s *Neighbours* cast-inspired mullet haircut was bad enough right now, without adding a pixie-cut fringe. Again.

The match smelled. I watched as the blue flames whooshed to life inside the oven. I stared down at the floor, the lino all cracked and warped, brown and yellow and patterned in – what was it – a little like a filigree? I think that was the word. I tried not to pick at it as I placed the chicken inside. I wondered what the other kids were doing after school. Maybe they were playing netball. Placing the heavy chicken inside, I closed the door, and just stared at the flames for a little bit. I looked at the brown wooden clock that hung above the sink. It was a bit crooked. Still, I made a mental note that I'd have to get the frozen three-vegie mix out of the freezer and start that in about an hour and 20.

In a little while, the smell of sadness in the air would be replaced.

Soon it would start to smell like hope. Well, it would smell like hope for a little while, at least. Maybe she would venture out of the dark room. Maybe she would make it to the mismatched dinner table with its cracked white top and slightly rusty silver legs and wooden chairs.

Maybe she would join us.

Maybe my little Sissy – my blonde-haired, blue-eyed Sissy – would not sit outside the door of that sad room, and defiantly eat the chicken on the floor as she begged through sobs for our mum to please come out.

Maybe, just maybe, the light would seep into the room, and the smell of sadness would start to disappear – at least for a while.

~~~~~~~

Do you remember? That little girl locked inside the corner of my mind was standing in protest at the edge of my bed. She was tough. She looked for the upswing. She looked for the good in people. She did not believe in quitting.

She was standing on my brown carpet, bare feet planted firmly. *Do you remember the smell?* She leaned forward. Remember what it was like to be responsible for Mum? How you promised that you would be THE mum, not my mum, or your mum. You know – *our* mum? Remember you promised to be different? Remember you promised that you would always fight? No matter what?

Damn. She was right.

I'd needed to do something.

I'd needed to phone a friend. I'd thought about who I wanted to phone. Jo? Lauren? Becs?

Ugly crying, I'd picked up my phone. Half under my doona in the middle of summer. Eyes puffy. Not knowing what the hell to do on the life front. Shit-scared that I had managed to stuff everything up. That I had fallen into working so hard, and being so strong, I was at risk of missing out on joy.

With one red-brown puffy eye, a slice of my puffy face still meekly on the pillow under the doona, I'd decided to FaceTime my friend and utter with a sob: "Becs…"

"Hi, chick… oh, no – whaaat's happened? Where are you? All I can see is your eye. Have you been crying?"

"I'm in bed."

It was 10 am when I'd called. I'm normally up and out at 5 am. This was not normal. I didn't do sleep-ins. Like, ever. Not in winter. Definitely not in summer.

I'd made the most horrendous sucking-snot-back-up-into-my-face sniff.

"Yesss…" she'd said. "Wait, *where* are you?"

"I think I've stuffed up everything. And I'm freaking out!"

"Have you hurt your back? Do you need to go for a massage? You could see Baker. He's an acupuncturist. You know, spiritually, the back is connected to all the people you are supporting, don't you?"

I was glad she couldn't see my whole face.

"Yes, but that's not it. I'm worried that I'm going to turn into my mum. There is nothing wrong with my (sob) life right (sob) now, but I am scared that I don't know how to find (sob) joyyy. I can't shake this feeling."

"Maybe it's retrograde."

Becs is quite spiritual. She knows about chakras, auras, speaking with dead people, Chinese astrology, normal astrology, retrogrades, clearing spaces, all that woo stuff. I am really just dipping my spiritual pinky toe back into the ocean. She's also my personal trainer and the person who introduced me to Baker. She kind of looks like a Nordic goddess. If Gwyneth Paltrow and Cameron Diaz hooked up and had a baby, it'd be Becs. Tall and tanned, blonde hair, spiritual and a bit kick-arse. Sparkly blue eyes. Makes a paper bag look like it came off a runway. And I have seen her wear a paper bag. For Halloween. She loves a dress-up.

Becs is also my friend who is very calming. We both talk each other up in confidence in different areas of our lives. I have helped her with her business and moving forward, letting go of what doesn't serve her. She has helped me with moving forward and letting go of emotions that don't serve me. In the middle is the normal banter about kids, travel, movies, books, drinking coffee, gaining weight, losing weight, doing detoxes, quitting coffee, having coffee withdrawals, eating paleo or vegan – all that jazz that you talk about with your girlfriends. She's one of my inner circle along with Jo, Jaq, Lauren, and my faux bro, Hector.

I kept blubbing. "Becs… I don't know what's wrong. My life is good, but I can't shake this feeling that it is all going to turn to shit. I don't know what to do."

"Belle, you have worked so hard; you are being hard on yourself. You need to create space for some fun and some joy, or you are going to burn out, honey! Think about what you would say to me if I was in your shoes!"

"I don't know what to do! I don't know how to fit it in with the kids and the business and keeping fit. I have heaps of friends, but at the same time I feel so isolated. Everyone seems to think I'm living this awesome life, and that I'm busy all the time, but I'm just busy working. The fun is just missing! It's work, work, work. Kids, kids, kids. Clean, clean, clean. What happened?"

Becs' tone had changed. For the first time during our friendship, she'd become direct and bossy.

"Stop! What are you doing right now?"

I'd heard her frustration with me. I'd needed to hear her frustration with me.

"Hiding under the doona," I admitted.

"Where are the kids?"

"They have gone camping with their dad and will be back tomorrow – why?"

"Right," she ordered, "get your bathers on, and get down the beach, and get in the bloody water. Not just your feet. You used to be a water baby and do stuff, Belle – you have got to get that fun back, no matter how worried you are about things. Get out there and dunk yourself to get rid of this energy you are carting around. Hand it over to the universe. You are better than this."

I'd never heard my nurturing friend go all tough love on me. Well, except for when we are training in the gym, but that is more physical. Her direct tone shocked me into action.

You need to move.

Listen to what Becs has said.

Pick your arse up.

Get out the door

Go to the beach.

Chase the joy, you big chicken.

Be brave. Go on a date. Show your kids what love looks like.

Chase the joy in life. Not just in work. Chase it down like a greyhound after a rabbit.

Everywhere.

A wave smashes me up the side. Again. I should know this by now, yet it still catches me off guard. My tears subside, as I look down into the water.

My body is far from a bikini body at the moment. I worked so hard to improve things last year then I spiralled out of control. I still exercised the same. But my eating? Even though I know all the right things to do for my body, that went out the window. That, plus stress, and things were definitely out of balance in one area.

I stare vacantly. In my mind, I really don't care. I'm on autopilot, doing what I have been told. It's not my first autopilot moment, either. It's also not my worst one.

I only live five minutes from the beach, so I'm lucky that going for a dunk in the ocean is not a big ask.

So here I am. Being pummelled by the green lady. A long way from my dreams of being some surf chick from 11 years old. And fighting to be a long way from turning into the mum I had from 11 years old.

I can't even remember the last time I actually enjoyed the ocean, let alone anything else that was not work – or kid-related and just for me – activities not completed out of necessity, but out of desire.

I mean, the ocean and I were besties for as long as I can remember before kids. Our relationship has ebbed and flowed.

The ocean was where I went after Mum died. The waves slapping me up the side of the head are making me think of what those death punches felt like. In particular, the first big death punch of January 1994.

Twenty-five years ago I grabbed the keys to my black death trap (but uber-cool) VW Beetle Convertible. I started to head to the door to go and see my mum.

She'd called earlier in the day to say I love you. I'd said I love you back and had organised to go and cook with her. I'd moved out of home into a small flat, so any cooking skills I could pick up were welcome. This was my third time out of home. The first time, she thought it was a good idea to send me to live in a caravan park at 16 (it wasn't). The second time, we'd had a fight and she had slapped me hard across the face, so I went to live with my best friend at the time and her family until things were repaired. Mum hadn't liked my view on her life choices. The goody-two-shoes child versus the rebellious and troubled parent who'd switched from finding God and being baptised to nightclubbing. With a vengeance. She'd apologise; I'd move home and try to help her.

That time, I'd moved out of my own accord – I thought it was the right thing to do. I was looking forward to cooking with her. She was quite the cook. It was how I first explored the world – Thai, Italian, Mexican, Hungarian, Indian, Egyptian and then, of course, the Aussie staple of meat and three veg. It was how my love of difference and diversity started.

My flat was tiny. I think it would fit into the living room and kitchen of the house I live in now. I had made this decision to move out for a few reasons. Not like the two times prior. The main one being, her depression was something I felt myself being sucked into, and I figured that maybe, just maybe, if I moved out, if I was no longer the go-to, the crutch, the 19-year-old trying to solve problems that I really had not the skills for, maybe Mum would fight. Maybe I would be in a better position to help her. I knew if I started to sit in the hole, in the dark, it wouldn't be good for either of us. I could feel myself being sucked in. Yet the guilt of that choice – even though I have worked to make my peace with it – still rears its ugly head from time to time in what-if moments. What if I had stayed?

God, how I wanted her to fight. To fight for herself, for her happiness. For our family. I wanted her to fight her depression. I'd tried – without the knowledge at the time – encouraging her to take up activities like golf, to get back into art, to choose what would make her happy. I'd prayed my arse off. That she would fight. That I would have the right answer to help her.

Yet when it came to being asked what she should do with her relationships, I told her what she wanted to hear over what I believed. I told her to choose what would make her happy – I don't know if that was the right thing to say. I just wanted her to be happy.

She was in the midst of moving out of our home and in with another man – that is a whole other story. Her life is a whole other story, really. It wasn't easy. There were packing boxes everywhere. Half her stuff was at one destination, half at another. Yet we still had this plan on January 12 to cook.

I walked to my door, only to be greeted by a knock. *Timing.* What if I had gone sooner? My energy, which was positive and full of hope in going to see Mum, soon shifted as I opened the door.

Something was wrong. Really wrong. There stood my stepdad with my younger sister.

"Hi! What's up? I'm just on my way to see Mum – I'm running late."

Something was wrong. Their faces looked wrong. My sister looked wrong. My stepdad looked wrong. His eyes red, his lip trembling amidst his bearded face. My sister stood behind him. Silent. Lights out. Dark. Scared. I didn't know they had already been punched. I didn't know I was about to be punched. I didn't know I was about to get in the ring with God and have my 19-year-old life, my house, my scrappy foundations, obliterated.

"Bee – you can't go…"

"Mum's dead."

"What?"

16

"Mum's dead, she's dead."

They hadn't even stepped inside my house. With those words, I felt the full force of the universe reach in and rip my heart out.

Death punch.

Like being winded.

Knocked backwards into my tiny flat.

Past the small, hand-me-down wooden lounge chairs covered in brown and cream tapestry. Past my bare walls. Back into my tiny kitchen where we had cooked spaghetti days earlier.

Death punch.

Where did all the air in my lungs just go? Where did all my thoughts go? I wasn't expecting this. I'd moved out of home two weeks ago. Wrong move.

I had walked back into a wall, and slid to the floor.

Death punch.

I couldn't breathe.

She'd lost her fight – and it had been a long one. Now I had to start mine.

Get back up. Back up off the floor.

Punch back.

Shock came first, then tears, then shock again, then not sleeping, not knowing what to do as I watched not only my own world crumble, but the people I loved crumble and disappear. Disappear into their own void, their own story and experience of grief and loss.

I tried, as best as I could, to stick the pieces of my broken family back together. My dad. My stepdad. Her potential husband number four. My younger sister. My older half-sister, who I was meeting, really, for the first time. My older half-brother – who had his own experiences.

Total clusterfuck.

Emotions ran high. My father's words – fuelled by scotch – were hurled over phone lines like Molotov cocktails as years of hatred, pain and hurt came bursting out of decades-held tongues.

None of them had been her emotional crutch at the end.

None of them had been charged with giving life advice to a woman who needed it from someone way more qualified than 19-year-old me. None of them had been the one to move out of home two weeks prior for fear of being sucked into the black hole of depression too. I knew if I stayed, I would end up unable to help. None of them carted the heaviness of guilt that came with her death.

I tried, as best as I could, to hold on tight to who I was, to put my wounds to the side, to pick up my wounded family and try, as hard and as heavy as it was, to move forward. Slowly.

I tried, as best as I could, to protect those I loved – not realising that as I carried the wounded with me, my own scars were forming underneath the armour. I mean, we don't know what we don't know.

I'm sure she didn't realise the impact of the death punch that her choice delivered. I'm sure I didn't realise the walls I would build and the fear of experiencing sadness I would develop in the process.

Conversations echo from one of her six brothers. I don't remember who. She was one of 14. Fred, maybe. Apparently I had worn my grief armour like a tailored suit.

"You seem to be coping well; you should go to the house and look for a suicide note. You should go and look for a will. You can pick out the coffin. Do you know if she wanted to be buried or cremated?"

"She told me she wanted to be cremated."

"We think it would be better if there was a place to go and visit."

"Okay, but she said she didn't want to be worm food."

"We think there should be an open casket. It might help some of those come to realise that she is not coming back."

"She never wanted to be viewed that way, but okay – if it will help."

I was charged with finding her make-up and lipstick. I was charged with going through her black A-Z pop lid telephone and address book. Calling her friends, one by one. Telling them she had died, one by one. Each dial of the round rotary phone dial feeling like it was part of the numbing process, as I'd wait for the number to circle back before I could dial the next 4, the next 1 or the next 9.

I had spoken to my dad to tell him that his behaviour was not appropriate. That I understood and knew over the years how much hurt and hatred there had been. That I had listened to it from them both on any given Sunday. I had to tell him not to ring my stepdad again, drunk, and tell him that he wished he was in the grave too.

I had to tell him to apologise. I had to chastise him, and tell him that because of his behaviour, he was not to come to the funeral. That it was best if his bitterness stayed away. That I had to make tough decisions.

I had to choose the church – should it be her church? It was kind of a basketball court-slash-shed where we prayed on a Sunday.

"I should find a nicer church…" I had told myself. Would I go to Hell for that? Would God punish me for choosing the older, fancier Catholic church over the simple Baptist one?

Their voices echo again.

"You can write the speech and do the eulogy."

I had walked past the casket, not looking. I didn't want to. I had walked to the pulpit. I had stared at the faces of her brothers, her father, her children, her friends, as I said my speech.

I had read my poem; got over my fear of public speaking. I had delivered the eulogy. I told myself that if I could do that at 19, I could do anything. I had stared at the front row, looking at my older sister, Witchy – the only new light I could see in all of this. My prodigal half-sister who I'd only really met once before at a bus station in Queensland when I was 10, maybe, and she was 19. The one who would, in time, remind me of love and laughter, and choosing living over existing in amongst this fantastical shit fight called death.

I had stared at the hole in the ground. The one where her body would stay in the fancy timber coffin I had helped to pick out. I watched her sink down into this final hole. It was horrible, that deep, dark hole. But it was not as dark and as deep as the one she battled, and not as dark and deep as the one she left behind, mud-like.

Time moved like mud. Stuck in grief mode. Occasionally, one of the 'adults' attempted to adult.

"Do you think you should all go and speak to a grief counsellor?"

"Why?"

Sissy was in denial.

I was looking at the shattered, fracturing mess.

Denial.

Punch back.

I had tried, as best as I could, to navigate all the horrid things that death can do to people.

Denial. Anger. Blame. Regret. Shame. Withdrawal. Abandonment. Rejection. Disconnection.

While some of my family were rooted firmly in denial, others disowned me for trying to protect who I loved – for fighting the good fight. Those once my allies, like my own biological father, drew lines where all forms of communication ceased. The man I loved, the man of magic, my 'every-other-weekend Dad', started to walk past me in Hay St Mall and looked through me with disappointment as though I was an empty scotch glass.

I had gone and sat at the beach where the blue wheat silos jut out of the horizon. I had sat there with my Mum's favourite non-alcoholic wine, concealed in a brown paper bag. I sat staring blankly at the green lady, took off my cross… and threw it at her as though I was spitting on someone or something I now loathed.

I was hurt. Deeply.

So I started a war with the God who had protected me as a child. The God I no longer understood.

I had watched my tiny cross – the source of my protection – sink to the bottom of the ocean. So I had sunk everything else, too. Way, way down into the depths, where dark things belong. I thought it was strength.

I didn't just lose my mum.

My dad, my younger sister, my stepdad – they all got lost in the haze and daze that the death punch delivered. Some, like my dad, lost for almost two years; some longer. Their memories (for those still alive) are different to mine. Some of them say it's a blur. Some of them placed her on a faultless, flawless pedestal. For me, 1994 is a crystal-clear, clusterfuck year with "No Rain" by Blind Melon playing on repeat as I drove between the funeral home, the house she had lived in, and the house she was moving to, looking for whatever I was tasked with looking for to make the burden a little easier on those I loved.

Because I loved them.

Because I chose to do it.

Because I had weathered different storms before.

And I had tried, as best as I could, to navigate the life I still had to live.

My 19-year-old world kept turning with the big, fat, gaping hole left behind from a death punch.

The green lady slaps me again, bringing me back to the present. I've always, always tried to look at my life as a gift. When things have happened, and I am still standing, I try (as much as it may seem like I am focusing on a loss right now) to remember the things that I can do because I am here. How lucky I am.

I have not lost a child.

I was not born in a third-world country where hunger and other basic needs are a struggle (hello, future aid worker me – life goal). I can walk, talk, eat, sleep, speak freely.

I can do good in this world.

I believe I was gifted these hard, tough lessons for a reason. That pain has purpose. If you allow.

Life is a gift. A choice. Something worth fighting for. So what is happening right now is just an ebb in the flow, right?

Maybe, just maybe, I can tell others who might be in my mum's position that, no, your absence would not make this world better. You need to be brave.

Fight for your light.

That, no, your loved ones don't just feel a death punch once, they feel it repeatedly.

Fight for their light.

That, yes, you are worthy, yes, you are loved, yes, you should punch back.

Yes, things are shitty and tough some days. We have a choice. Fall down, sure – we are human.

Then...

Get.

The fuck.

Back.

Up.

And for the love of God, for the love of life, for the love of those you think don't need you – believe me, yes, in 25 years, you are still missed, still loved, still wished for that you had fought against the darkness one more day. Still found courage and bravery.

If you break an arm, you go and seek help. You don't leave your broken limb dangling there in an odd shape.

If your thoughts are broken, your beliefs are broken, your love of life is broken... same goes. Go and seek help. Friends, counsellors, professionals. Asking for help is uncomfortable, but important.

Because you are worthy of fighting for you.

Twenty-five years on... I still look for all the good things in the world.

Twenty-five years on... I still feel that death punch when I allow its memory to crystallise. Today, it's serving as a reminder.

Twenty-five years on... I still want to be a fighter, a warrior, because I believe that life is a choice worth living, and that you are worthy. That I am worthy.

That I can just 'be' in the ocean.

I used to be out here in the sea all the time. Either sailing around in it, diving into it, paddling on it or boogie boarding in it.

I had always wanted to learn to surf it... I just felt too uncool to ever do that, having been a nerd pretty much my whole life. Plus, we never had the money.

Maybe that is something I can do this year... Finally learn to surf. Maybe, just maybe, I will learn, no matter the feelings that I shouldn't be learning. Maybe I'll talk to Lauren and Jo about this later. See what the last thing was that they wanted.

So here I am. Another wave whacks me up the side of the face. But at least the snot is being washed away now.

Clarity is washing away the chaos of pressure that has started in my mind.

I start thinking, as the ocean moves me back and forth and my thoughts fall in line with the tide. And I start realising that some things have to change. That even though my life is, for all intents and purposes, pretty good, it's not full. The fun factor went missing. The tide of joy went out somewhere along the way.

I became 'mum Belle'. The rush of waves to the shore. The undertow that comes with motherhood. Juggling the demands of two small kids on my own. Trying desperately to create meals that will be eaten and appreciated instead of having noses turned up at them in disgust (except for the kid faves of vegetarian lasagne and pumpkin soup, until all of a sudden no one likes it anymore). I had this joy for cooking, and it slowly just vanished. It turned into a thankless job. Without another adult around, it just gets you down after a while. I keep on top of school admin (which feels like a full-time job in itself), and secretly ferret copious amounts of toilet roll artwork that, while beautiful, needs to go to the recycle bin lest we end up on a special episode of *Hoarders: Homework and Craft* or something. I work to get them outside doing fun stuff, only to be met with looks of disdain.

I became boring 'work Belle'. Trying to fit all the business stuff in around school hours – I mean, that is how I designed it. But sometimes I miss having that other person in my life to share the load, and just give a big man hug to say, "It's okay, babe, you've got this." Actually, I miss a big man hug from any adult – even though half my family have been dead for 10 years or more, I still miss them. Their absence can become a big presence.

And my friends and my community just see me as 'busy Belle'.

"Oh, we just know how busy you are, so we don't invite you to anything."

It's not on them – that's on me. That's the energy I've been giving off. And, truth be told, with all the kid stuff, mum stuff and work stuff, I *am* busy. But that doesn't mean it is the best use of my life. I don't want to be an Energizer bunny and then die. That would be shit.

I became 'scared to be vulnerable and brave Belle'. I became 'standing and telling women in the workshops that I run each February that there is great strength in vulnerability, but not being fully vulnerable and open myself Belle'. I mean, on the dating front, I have not even approached a date and I've been single for going on three years now. I'm not walking my bloody walk in a big enough way! I'm so scared of being sad and turning out like mum and my kids experiencing my childhood. That's not what I want for them.

I want to live the crap outta my life. I feel responsible to do so. I mean, here I am in the ocean. My mum, my dad, my older sister – they aren't here to do life anymore. Nor is Dixie, my mother-in-law.

I feel the pull of another wave, turning to duck-dive under again. My timing is off, and I get washing-machined, hanging onto my bikini bottoms that really need replacing.

Bloody Becs. She was right. I did need this. The shock of the water, and being out in the world instead of stuck in my house (I don't even know why

I own a house, the suburban 4x2 dream was never my dream), does something. It shifts something. I mean, I know how precious life is. I've been brave in lots of different ways.

It's time to be brave again. Even if I'm gonna feel like a super dork.

I swim back to the shore. As I do, I notice a few flags up on the beach where a surf coach is. He is very weathered – kind of like Crocodile Dundee meets Kelly Slater with a side of Mark Ruffalo. I imagine him saying, "That's not a board, *this* is a board." He's a salty version – I can't guess his age, late fifties maybe? In place of an Akubra hat he has a mop of greying sandy curls and piercing blue eyes. Surf Dundee!

A couple of flags are up to signal board hire, so I make a mental note to do something about this long-held desire to learn how to surf.

Am I too old? Should I be too old? Am I too fat? Am I too... anything?

I try to fight the story that I have labelled myself as a dorky nerd and that I should accept my lot in life.

I grab my boogie board and head out to catch a wave. I'm sure I have my thinking face on. I can feel my eyebrows furrowed as I question how hard I am on myself. Why it's easier to be kinder to others than it is to be kind to myself. Why I should even give a shit about whether I am being judged by others... I mean, this is my life, not theirs, right? I don't know the last time I did something I loved. I mean, I love my job, my kids, my friends. But joy-based love – love that is not linked to being a good mother or worker or any of the other roles – where the only outcome that you are focused on is that feeling of joy and freedom. Where the joy is just for you. Not mechanical joy – flowy joy.

I've been out in the ocean for a while now. The thought that Becs is right sinks deep into my soul. It has made a difference. I feel the shift. I know I need to do this more. I know I need to be a little more brave with my life, in fully living it. In being vulnerable and getting back out there into the unpredictable waters, where I might fail and get hurt. I've put some protective walls up for a while. I guess I needed the reminder that maybe I need to crack things open in some areas again. I decide to turn emotions back on, even though my survival mode is to switch them off again.

I head back in with a little more clarity and start to think about if I am to have a 'Year of Bravery', walking my walk instead of just talking my talk, who I can call upon.

The sand has warmed up, and I stare down at my toes as I hotfoot it back to the car. I realise I need to make some changes. I've got some unanswered questions in my life. I've got some stuff I want to try to experience. I've got a life I need to actually live. I mean, three dead family members should be enough to make you want to live, yet even then, you still need an emotional kick in the arse every so often to remind you that you are here to live, and they are not, so best you go do shit that they cannot. Best that you actually live!

I think of my closest friends who will be good at keeping me on track.

There's Becs: spiritual and fitness arse-kicker. Jo: super honest, no BS, tells it like it is –probably Grand Master of the Universe arse-kicker. Lauren: a vulnerability role model to me, especially with mental health. I love how open she is with her own story on social media. Jaq: who I've supported while she was brave in getting back out into date land, and I know will support me if and when I need to call upon her. Actually, they will all support me – we all support each other. We all bring something different. I am very blessed on the friend front. We are there for each other even if we can see each other not making the best decision. We don't abandon one another, and we tell the truth at the same time. Could not ask for a better bunch of core friends.

As I arrive home, still wet, hair all matted with gobs of sand, and looking about a dollar twenty, I stay in my wet bathers and get ready to make a phone call. Lauren.

We've started talking about doing some stuff together this year. I figure she might be a good person to take to the upcoming trip to Vegas for a business mastermind later in the year.

I committed to Vegas last year to expand my business connections, and to try to create my own Cheryl Strayed moments of hiking around the Grand Canyon. I also figured that I wanted to tick an item off my list and drive from LA to Vegas, just for the experience. I didn't care if anyone came along or not – I just thought it would be good to experience.

Lauren knows me as this strong type of person, so I start testing my vulnerability out with her. She is a new person for me to do this with. Becs and Jo are aware, yet when it comes to the mental health space, I really admire how raw and real Lauren has been. I see what she does as incredibly brave, so figure she would be a great person to do some brave stuff with. In some ways, she's like my vulnerability role model.

"Lauren, I have to be honest with you. I'm not doing that great at the moment, mentally – I know that people see me as this strong, independent person, but the truth is, I need to have some more fun."

"Oh, Belle! Do you want me to come over?"

"No, I'm good – I'm just clearing my head… But I would like to catch up and see if you want to come to the beach with the kids and go for a boogie board with me in the next couple of days."

"Okay. Just warning you, I'm not really a beach person, but okay. Will be good to get the kids out of the house."

"You don't like the beach?"

"I like the beach, but not the ocean. On account of there is a huge amount of fucking sharks there."

"I never think about the sharks when I go to the beach. Except when I see the drones or the surf helicopter out patrolling the beach, then I do. But hey, I've just got to swim faster than you and I'll be fine, hahaha."

Lauren is not amused. "So, aside from shark repellent, what do I need to bring?"

"Definitely sunscreen, given how super-white you are."

She is very Cate Blanchett crossed with Zooey Deschanel, plus a Kiwi accent, so raven locks, porcelain skin and a beautiful heart. Somehow a lot of my friends are on the rock god spectrum... and then there's me, the token wallflower dork who has somehow infiltrated the pack. I mean, even Lauren's husband looks like he belongs in a band. I've seen pics. They are uber-cool.

"Yep," she says. "Do you have spare boogie boards? I don't know if I have enough for the kids."

"I've got a couple, but bring yours down anyway. Want to go from my house or meet me near the surf club?"

"I'll come with you. I'm not familiar with that beach."

"What bitch?"

"Are you making Kiwi jokes?"

"Yep, sorry! I love your accent. Make sure you wear your jandals."

"Yeah and you make sure you wear your thongs. On your feet, you dag."

"Okay, see you on Saturday at 10. I'll bring snacks."

Saturday rolls around and we head to the beach. The kids are here reluctantly. They'd rather stay home watching other people open Kinder Surprise eggs on YouTube, and it is becoming a problem that we both talk about. Getting kids outside so they don't turn into techno couch zombies, disconnected from everyone. Especially with the sun shining and the weather being as nice as it is.

Funnily, though, once the kids are out here, they have a good time. They start building sandcastles and digging tidal pools at the edge of the shoreline.

I yell out to them, "Hey, kids, us mums are going to catch a few waves. The bigger kids are in charge while we do this, okay?"

Abby, my daughter, the nurturer and sometimes bosser of her brother, is more than happy to do this. She is also quick to ask if it is a paid gig, as she has paid attention while my business journey has been happening.

"I'll do it for $10," she says.

Before I get a chance to say, no, you will do it for love and because you are part of the family, Lauren pipes in with a counter-offer.

"I'll give you five bucks."

"Seven."

"Six, and we have a deal – final offer."

"Okay, deal. Blame Mum – she taught me to negotiate!"

I look at Lauren, and realise I should have warned her about my daughter's entrepreneurial spirit.

"You didn't have to do that," I tell her. "Sorry, she was too quick!"

"Oh, sorry! I didn't realise. She's quite the entrepreneur – wonder where she gets it from!"

"Yes, that's true… She's also just learned what commission is, so watch she doesn't try and flog you something else to make a buck."

"What does she put her money towards?"

"Generally mints. Or these stupid squishy things that the dog eats. Anyway, you ready to catch a wave?"

Then, for the first time in I don't know how long, we – *the mothers* – head into the surf. With boogie boards. We head out into waist-deep water, just beyond the sandbar where the waves are breaking, and catch waves. While the big kids sit on the shore with the little kids and make a sandcastle. And the kids don't die. Winning! Totally winning!

There is a light easterly breeze, making the waves hold their form really nicely, giving us a good run back into the shore.

We catch each other's faces and see the joy, sharing thoughts like *Why are we always sitting on the shoreline?* We head back out again and again, until the seagull cries of "Muuum! Muuum! Muuum!" echo out and we head back in.

Those thoughts of 'why' soon turn into words as we sit back on the beach towels and resume our normal role of watching the kids and watching for, well, anything. Being a sentry 24/7 is tiring work, when you factor in everything else. Not that we want to put our kids at risk – it just seems that we have become hypervigilant these days.

I turn to Lauren. "Hey, do you ever feel like we are missing out? Like we are constantly on watch, but the dads don't seem to be? I mean, I'm not meaning to diss dads, but they seem to be out there having fun, so why aren't we?"

I signal to a couple of dads out in the surf with their kids on surfboards, and the wives sitting on their beach towels, just watching. Maybe enjoying the quiet. Maybe being a sentry on the lookout for sharks or rips, or a kid about to drown. Like us.

"Yeah, I was just thinking the same. We are always on the lookout."

"Watch out for sharks."

"Watch out for stranger danger and sexual predators."

"Watch out for online bullying. Watch out for in-real-life bullying."

"Watch out for weirdos online. Watch out for feeding your kids the right food."

"Watch that you stay body positive and don't talk shit about yourself in front of your kids, and balance allowing carbs while trying to get them to eat kale. I mean, I can't get my kids to eat kale! Carrots are a big enough challenge."

"I hear ya. Watch out for opportunities, and make sure you give them, and can do all the running around to make it happen."

"Watch out for behaviours. Watch out that they don't turn out to be four-foot-tall arsehats."

"Watch out that you give the right amount of freedom, while watching out that you maintain the right level of control, because lo and behold, if something happens to a kid while you are watching out, you will be to blame."

"Yep!" I pause. "I have an idea!"

"Me too! We should go do stuff," Lauren echoes my thoughts.

"Yeah! We should. We should be brave and try new things. I could really use your help with being brave in some areas of my life."

"And maybe we can encourage others to get off the sidelines with their lives. Or maybe they will be brave, too."

"I'm thinking the same thing," I admit.

"What's on your list?" Lauren asks.

"Well, I know I have to get back out there in the dating world, which freaks me right out… but on a more practical and less-scary-for-me side, I want to learn to surf."

As I say this, I signal to Surf Dundee, who is setting up his flags to peg out where he is about to teach a couple of middle-aged Asian tourists how to surf.

Lauren comes out with, "I want to try pole dancing."

"I want to try to overcome my fear of frogs. Hey, you should come to Vegas with me for this business mastermind! I'm going to drive from LA to Vegas, and then go hike the Grand Canyon. Do you want to come?"

"I'm scared of spiders… maybe I can overcome that. I don't think I'm ready for the mastermind. I'm worried I'm not at your level."

"We are never ready. And all the more reason to come is to surround yourself with people who are further along. I mean, if I want to learn to surf, I'll go ask that guy over there, not the 13-year-old grom out on his board with raging teenage hormones. You should come! We could go on a mumventure! No kids! No husbands. Not that I have one of those. But we could see what it is like to be Belle and Lauren the persons instead of Belle and Lauren the mums or Belle and Lauren the workers, or wives, or any other roles that we play."

"I'll have a think about it and talk to Logan."

"Okay, well let me know. I'm going to book flights soon. You don't have to come on the Grand Canyon thing, but it's on my list to go and sit on a rock and just take in the view. I do have to warn you, though, when I say I'm going to hike the Grand Canyon for the whole day, I mean the whole day. I want to make the most of the chance to just be in awe of the world and see if anything happens to my brain. You know, like getting clarity, or a message."

"Okay, well, let's see. So, what about the dating thing? Are you going to get back out there?"

"Yeah, I need to. It's one of my fears, but I've been thinking on it for a while, and I have got to work up the courage to do something about it."

"Oooh! I can be your wing woman!"

"Dude, I am so rusty, I'll probably give some poor guy tetanus! I do want to be brave and move forward for happiness. Right now, I know what working smart looks like, I know what exercising looks like and eating kale looks like, but I'm afraid I'll forget what love looks like. I'll end up in an apartment in the city wearing fake leather pants, with grey hair that is dip-dyed pink, being eaten by a thousand cats."

"Belle! You won't get eaten by cats!"

"It's a possibility. I'd rather die exploring. What should we do on our list first?"

Together, we start brainstorming some ideas of things that will push us out of our comfort zones and break us back into 'we the people' – no matter how awkward or embarrassing it might get.

As we pack up the kids and head back to the car, sandy towels, sandy boogie boards and sandy butts in tow, we make a plan to catch up in a week to talk about Vegas and other plans. I make a mental note to jot down on my whiteboard the items on our list (plus a couple of my own).

- Try pole dancing
- Learn to surf
- Face fears of frogs and/or spiders
- Hike the Grand Canyon
- Be okay with feeling everything including sadness and rejection
- Find out about the abuse
- Find out about this whole Baker thing
- Tell the kids I'm going to start dating

- Go on an actual date
- Be okay being naked
- Be vulnerable
- Be okay. No matter what

―――――

Getting home, my hair is in its usual post-beach state, all matted up and salty. I need a shower with a ton of conditioner to undo the sand dreads, but my kids are out the front under the sprinklers as a way to wash off the salt from the beach, enjoying the early-morning heat of summer, so I am happy to have five minutes to chat to Becs on the phone. I want to thank her.

"Becs! Hey, I need to thank you for your tough love last week. I've never heard you be bossy like that before – well, except when you are making me lift dumbbells over my head. I honestly think you may have just saved my life."

"Oh, hun, that's okay. I knew it would help you. The ocean is great for clearing your mind, and literally washing any negative energy off and away."

"Well, I should explain. I don't mean that I was at risk of suicide. I'd never do anything like that on account of Mum…"

"It must be close to the anniversary of her death, right?"

"Yeah, it's in two days, but I don't think that was the cause of the funk."

"I don't either. But you need to make space for fun, Belle. I was worried about you last week. Jo was worried about you, too. She rang me."

"I'm so lucky with the friends I have. But I do need to explain. I think you saved my life in terms of inspiring me to step up and be brave with it. I mean, superfuckingbrave. I need to be vulnerable again, because I think we both know that while I have this happy, bubbly exterior, I haven't been living. Fully."

"No," Becs agrees, "you've been busy working and looking after kids. Which is fine, but what is the point of all of it if you aren't getting to have fun? Come on, you teach us that. To work on *your* terms. You've gotta get back out there, Belle. It's been, what? Two years?"

"Two and a half. Well, anyway. That day that you told me to get out in the ocean... I think you saved my life. I'm going to live this year and be brave. Promise."

"Well, you are brave already, just look at the life you have lived."

"I know, but I don't want to be brave in terms of being resilient and surviving shit and making changes. I need to be brave in the way of being vulnerable and going after joy. Anyway, Becs, I just want you to know that I love you, and I appreciate the reality slap. It has shifted something for sure."

"Okay, I'll see you soon. Gym sessions start up again soon."

"Oh, and just quickly, how's Baker?"

"He's okay. He left his job, and is working on his business, so he's finding it hard to adjust. Why do you ask?"

I become guarded with my close friend, not wanting her to know that I might have a little crush on our mutual friend. A crush that I am trying *not* to have. At all.

"Oh, just this time of year, with job changes and stuff, sometimes it can be tricky mentally, especially for men, so just a little welfare check. That's all. See you Wednesday for leg day, gorg!"

As I hang up the phone, I stare out my window to the kids racing around under the sprinklers. I can't believe I am here. It's been quite a few years. I'm a long way from Melbourne. A long way from my old corporate life. A long way from working 50–60 hours a week. A long way from those awkward boss conversations you have to have.

Yep. I'm going to re-embrace my awkwardness in the spirit of vulnerability and bravery. Bring it, universe. Bring on item one on the list. Lauren's choice: pole dancing. Yikes!

2

FEBRUARY

*M*y phone rings. It's Jo. "Hey!" she says. "Have you done that stripper thing yet?"

I love tech. I love FaceTime. She's outside in a paddock; I see her little house to the left. The phone is propped against who knows what, as she tends to a little fire that she is cooking on. In the background, I see Claire, her young daughter, race inside and grab the fat, rust-coloured chicken that has wandered in.

I watch my friend. Unruly long hair. Salt-and-pepper flecks, like the beaches she fossicks on, at her temples. Bare, hobbity feet. A jumper. Some type of apron. Pyjama pants. Pretty sure she's also braless. I watch her move back and forth with a pot. She's pretty resourceful. She's the person I would want around if a zombie apocalypse happened. The woman knows how to forage. Knows how to make stuff. Knows how to make me laugh. Knows how to shoot from the hip. I love her.

Most honest. Most loved. Most missed. Jo. A little bit Kate Winslet. A little bit Chelsea Handler. And according to some old guy on a flight she took, a bit John Lennon. She is a lot Jo. One of a kind.

We are the kind of friends that can call upon each other in any situation – 2 am, 2 pm, doesn't matter. She is a little more direct than Lauren or Becs. Actually, a lot direct. No filter. I wouldn't change it for the world. Real honesty and real truth are so rare; I'm super-lucky that my closest with the mostest ticks this box.

In a world where people get so tied up in not wanting to offend people, they trade elements of truth and authenticity for saving face and social grace. Jo still does social grace, and her country wiles and private school education see her turn out amazing cakes, conversation and cups of tea while wearing pearls with gumboots, but she is also one of my most loved friends who I can talk to about anything.

There really is no off-limit subject. "You shouldn't wear that top – it makes you look pregnant, and you're not." "What type of vibrator do you own? – What?! You don't have one? (snort laugh) You should get one!" "Have you tried having toast with ricotta cheese, fresh figs, ground pepper and Persian fairy floss?" "What's happening on the chap front?" And that could all occur in the space of 15 minutes – not separate conversations at all.

"That stripper thing? Oh, you mean the pole-dancing fitness thing?"

"Yeah, whatever."

"Yes. OMG. Talk about embarrassing, Jo. Have you ever met someone who made your jaw drop with their hotness, coolness and just all-round happiness (might be male or female), and then you don't see them for quite some time, and the next time you find yourself in the room with them, your brain, your whole being, just thinks they are equally amazing and equally you want them to rip all your clothes off against a wall in some '90s *Ally McBeal*-type steamy fantasy? All of a sudden, the lights are turned back on. And, like a mouse, you want to scurry away and hide, but you can't?"

"Well, not for a while, but yeah. I get it. Bit like if you meet a celebrity and then you go all stupid. What's that got to do with pole dancing?"

"Ugh. Well, I ended up injured and facedown in my mum undies in front of the rock god of hotness. I think I might have a crush."

She moves back, front and centre to the phone, bending down and eyeballing me over FaceTime. "When you say mum undies, please say you mean like the good date-night ones, not the sagging, used-to-be-white-but-are-now-that-kind-of-waste-water-grey Bonds ones."

I make a face that tells her it was the latter, not the former, my eyebrows raised, lips pulled together in dork face mode. My awkwardness showing. I nod.

"What's his name? Are you going to go on a date? What's he do? Is he any good?"

I start to laugh. The questions are rapid-fire.

"Slow down. Baker. No. Acupuncture. Yes. Becs recommended him. I met him last year."

"Oooh. If you are going to date, let's give them code names. What can we call this one. Is he hot?"

"Um. Yes. Just a bit. A lot a bit."

"Hot Hands."

"Explain?"

"Well, he's an acupuncturist, so he's using his hands on you?"

"Correct."

"And he's hot. So I'm calling him Hot Hands."

This is pretty accurate. If you put Chris Hemsworth and Bradley Cooper in a genetic blender, and add a bit of labrador-like, happy-go-lucky positivity, you'd produce the beautiful man candy that is Baker. Tall. Surfy-looking. Funny. I'd forgotten how hot he actually was since meeting him at a fundraising event that Becs had invited me to. Becs doesn't know I have a crush on him. I haven't told her.

"So, tell me – what happened? Take me back over the past week since we chatted."

"Well, Lauren and I went pole dancing. Remember how I trained for the bikini competition last year?"

"Yeah – didn't you stand on a piece of Lego or something and do an injury and get taken out?"

"Yep. Anyway, I thought because of the bikini comp and having to wear the six-inch plastic stripper heels for posing, I had an idea as to how hard this would be. I mean, stripper heels are hard enough to walk and practise striking a pose in. Dancing in them, Jo – that is next level. Plus, Bears (my son) told his very Catholic kindergarten teacher in news that he watched his mum and her friend pole dance on the weekend."

Jo snort laughs. "That's funny. Wish I'd seen his teacher's face. Okay, so who'd you train with? Anyone I'd know?"

"I don't know if you'd know her. Our instructor's name was Nikki. She attended one of the Mumpreneur workshops last year, and she got into pole fitness after being diagnosed with a terminal cancer, non-Hodgkin lymphoma. Pole fitness for her was a way of finding that fun again, her femininity, and her strength to look after her body and really live life. Anyway, Jo, spinning around on a pole takes a lot of strength. And grace."

"Yeah, you don't have a load of grace, I'd imagine. I've seen you dance. Hahaha."

"True. If attempting to walk in stripper heels while I trained for the bikini comp was awkward, trying to spin around the pole and look like I was worthy of Benjamins should the need arise in Vegas, well, that was not going to happen. The basic moves of holding the pole and spinning around is not a sexy look for me."

"Some people think goofballs are hot," Jo points out. "I mean, I get people commenting on my feet on Insta, so there is something for everyone. Do you have footage?"

"Yeah, somewhere. It ain't pretty. My face looks more like, 'Oh crap, how do I get off this thing?' Plus, I'm carrying about 20 kilos more than I'd like right now. You know when you go to a park and you see a little kid stuck on a roundabout for their first time, and they can't figure out how to get off?"

"Yeah, I've totally seen that before."

"Well, that would be me on a pole... Add that to the list of things I won't make money doing. That, and being a parking valet."

"I've seen your parking. It's crap."

"I know. Anyway, I don't know how women who do this as a paid gig don't get dizzy and fall into the crowd. They have skills, man. So Nikki walks around the pole with grace and ease. Lauren seems to get it, too. Nikki suggests trying an inversion, where basically you flip upside down and spin around on the pole. She makes it look super-easy. Lauren follows suit, and flips. Me... not so much. There is a lot of me to flip right now, and at best, I get to halfway before conceding defeat and feeling muscles start to scream with joy that they weren't going to be doing this again."

"So then what?"

"Well, it'd be fair to say that my body had a delayed response to realising just what it had attempted. I'm not made of Gumby rubber, hey. Turns out I'm made of sore muscles and sciatic nerves that are starting to ping. Have you had this before?"

"Sciatica? No, why, what's it feel like?"

"It kinda feels like someone has stuck needles... no, wait, not needles, blunt butter knives, into the back of your legs to the point that sitting, moving or even lying down flat brings you to tears."

If you asked me to make a list of worst pains I have experienced in my life, sciatica would probably have a first-place tie with the kind of toothache where you know you are going to end up financing your dentist's next trip to the Bahamas. Business class. Yep, I rate that pain over childbirth, breaking my arm twice and having appendicitis. Why? Because it can be around for a day before you treat it, and it really does bring you to tears just attempting to do simple things. Even lying flat can hurt. It's awful, shooting pain, where if you keep moving, it's okay.

I'm not a fan of taking any type of painkiller – I won't even take Panadol (including with the toothache thing). I'll look for a natural solution first every time. Drink loads of water. Try rolling around on one of those big foam rollers. Try stretching, hot yoga – anything.

"So how'd you end up seeing Hot Hands?"

"This is so embarrassing. Becs recommended him when I told her I'd done an injury. I didn't even think about it. I hadn't seen him in ages – not since I first met him at the Gatsby event from last year, so I just flicked off a text hoping he could fix everything."

Me: *Hey, Baker, it's Belle. I've done my sciatic and am hoping you've got space.*

Bakes: *Yep. Can you hold out until Monday @ 9.30?*

Me: *Yep. Thanks so much – I'm in mega pain (big sobby emoji).*

Bakes: *(Thumbs up emoji) Get some heat on it until I see you.*

I think back to when I first met Baker Cartwright, aka Bakes (you know how some people have last names for first names, and then, being Aussie, we shorten their name to a nickname, and then end up making it longer?). So Bakes, short for Baker, or if you are really good friends with the guy, Bakesey – because that's what we do – and I met at one of those network events. The Gatsby fundraiser.

Becs had invited a group of her mutual friends to attend, about a year ago. Now, I'm a dork. I can speak in front of crowds for business and workshops, no problem. Give me a room full of beautiful people and a styled event, and I retract into the surroundings like a sand crab hiding from my kids at the beach. Situational introvert.

I'd heard her talk about him before, at bootcamps, and just assumed that he was gay. Group training conversations had been peppered with comments like, "Oh, he's like one of the girls. He works as a teacher but has an acupuncture business on the side. We met at a wellbeing expo. He's called me to come and get a spider out of his studio before. I can't believe he screamed. Ask him for a good fake tan recommendation. He's not happy in his job and is thinking of going to study again, but who knows."

Mentally, I had created a picture of someone who was quite effeminate. Fit, without a hair out of place. I pictured someone like the character of Jack McFarland from *Will and Grace*, but with more of a Will body.

Man, was I wrong.

Dressing up and going where the cool people are is a big, fat anxiety red flag. Actually, red flag, neon lights and possibly Becs popping up and singing "Loser" and pointing at moi.

Dress to impress causes me stress! I'm most comfortable in either facilitator mode (work mode) or casual, go-do-stuff mode – read jeans, shift dresses for a BBQ, flip flops or activewear. I don't do fancy. Like, ever.

Anytime you say to me "event" or "dress to impress", my anxiety kicks into overdrive as I flashback to that nerdy high-school girl who thought a Hobbytex jumper with an eagle painted on the front worn with bubblegum jeans was cool. It wasn't.

I'd organised a dress, which was probably not the right style for me. I'd gone *Great Gatsby* nerd: horn-rimmed glasses, hair set, nerves in need of more than some deep belly breathing to walk into the room. Nerves in need of a vodka martini. Neeerrrrves – argh!

Either way, it was a cause close to home – raising funds for mental health awareness.

Even just going to this event, for me, was about feeling awkward. Funny. I tend to think of myself as an extrovert on the work front, but I'm probably a situational extrovert, really… And for this situation, I was nooo extrovert. Confidence completely gone.

I'd turned up to find the table with Becs, only to realise I'd landed flat bang on the #rockgodsquad table. All Becs' friends (except me) looked super-hot. If they were anything like Becs, I was sure they were lovely.

Lovely and hot. I didn't know how I'd ended up there. Social super-dork me had gatecrashed the adult cool table.

My heart raced. Thanks, internal chit-chat anxiety. I considered turning around and leaving. Internally, I thought I was going to vomit.

I was not far from wrong, walking off to the ladies' bathroom so I could hyperventilate in a cubicle for five minutes while staring at some random ad for doggie daycare. Emerging from the safety of the bathroom, I made a beeline for an event photographer – but not for photo opportunities. For safety.

I don't mind finding other solo workers. Tackling one new person socially has always been a little less daunting. Start small, and then tackle the table of beautiful people. I wasn't quite sure why social bravery was harder. Work bravery had never been a problem.

It was all my shit, all my insecurities – it was nothing to do with the rock god squad.

As I chatted to the photographer, I confessed that my anxiety was at an all-time high. The photographer, in turn, confessed that he liked being behind a lens, his creative security blanket that provided a buffer between him and people. It was nice to be twinning on the anxiety front, not so isolated and alone.

Offering to be the assistant for the evening, I confessed that I was shit at taking selfies, but I could probably get names and do that bit.

We laughed.

We joked.

The photographer, Phil, said, "Good luck – I'm going to take some food photos in the kitchen." Bye, social security blanket.

With proceedings about to start, I had no choice but to take my seat. On the table, there were literal mind games (maybe the right word is 'puzzles'). They were there to represent the complexity of our brains, our emotions, and to be a little bit of lighthearted fun.

Nervously I introduced myself to the rock god squad. As I did, another tall, rockstar-looking type came over and sat right next to me.

You know when you wonder what will happen if you ever meet a famous person, and you think you will act cool, but the reality is you will completely dork out and not be able to speak because somehow their energy and beauty has a power which renders you an idiot who can't even introduce themselves?

Well, that happened.

"Hey, I'm Baker!"

Oh shit, where do I look? Where's Phil!? Why is this dude talking to me?

"Hi, I'm Belle."

Cue the awkward silence.

"Um, so do you know anyone else on this table?" I stammered. "I know Becs, but that's about it."

I struggled to maintain eye contact. It felt like I was looking into the sun on a hot summer's day – all warm and glorious, yet also at risk of my retinas burning out.

Plus, I feared I might accidentally spit on him when I talked. You know, when you see like a miniscule spit drop come flying out of your mouth and you wonder if it has hit their visual range, but you can't Mr Miyagi it with a chopstick and catch it or anything, so you just have to hope it doesn't hit them on the face, or if it does, that it's so feather light it's not felt?

I'm sure I must have been coming off as unfriendly, but I was having a panic attack. *I'm so out of social practice. Oh God.*

I started actively fidgeting with the long string of pearls I was wearing as a way to channel my nervous energy. The way I was fidgeting, you'd have thought I had decided to count a rosary or something...

Then, to my horror, the string of pearls broke. Slow-motion, accidental spit-like, I watched in horror as pearls bounced off the table, down cleavages, into cocktails, and Becs caught one with her left hand with her spiritual ninja reflexes. She smiled, winked and returned to her conversation, placing the pearl on top of the bread roll she was not going to eat. Yep. I was in my own personal dork hell with all these cool people.

Baker stared at me, amused. I blushed terribly.

"Well," he said, "I know Alex and Lana, and I normally just see the back of Becs."

I watched the expression burst like a folded paper fan at the corner of his eyes as he smiled. I like lines on men. They look good. *Wonder if he has whitened his teeth? Man, they are super-white against his tan.* I tried focusing on his whole face.

He squirmed. "Ummm – do I have something in my teeth?"

"Oh, no, sorry, they are super-white. Sorry. So, what do you mean, the back of Becs?"

"She's a client of mine. I spend more time looking at her hamstrings and sticking needles in them than looking at her face. Those things get so tight, I could probably play a tune with my needles on them... she'd probably punch me if I did that, though."

Despite her spiritual woo side, Becs was super-fit. Like *Ninja Warrior*-candidate fit. I'd been friends with her for three years, training with her on a Thursday, religiously. She had seen me at one of my troughs when I became a single parent, commonly referred to as the 'squirrel cheeks' era, and she had seen me get back to a crest when she helped me train for a bikini competition... and the blow-out that lead to gaining back weight again. She'd seen the highs and the lows, and was way more than a PT in my mind. Given the height of her heels that evening, though, I could see why her hamstrings might be guitar-worthy.

"Needles?"

"Yep. I'm an acupuncturist in the Northern Beaches. Been doing it for about 20 years."

"Oh, really? Best stay away from me, then. I've accidentally taken an acupuncturist out before."

"What, like on a date?"

Huh, I wish, jellyfish! "No... bit more embarrassing than that. I'd been training for a bikini competition."

"A bikini competition? Like, with all the muscles and stuff?"

"Yeah. But I didn't want to get super-muscly. Just the first level. Bikini."

"Why?"

"Oh, it's a body confidence thing... I'd rather not get into it."

"So what's so embarrassing?"

"Well, turns out I am not that tough when someone sticks acupuncture needles into the sole of my left foot to release a trapped nerve. Like I said, I had been training for a bikini comp, and man, I can tell you that those girls have immense discipline and focus – especially mental. The easy part was the physical training. The hard part was the mental side of things... and walking and posing in plastic stripper heels."

"So why did you do it?" Baker asked.

His eyes were intense, and I stared at my plate, picking up the remaining stray pearls and putting them in a water glass, moving it to the middle of the table so I didn't accidentally pick it up and try to drink from it.

Reluctantly, I tried to explain that I'd set it as a goal for myself to try to build up body confidence and try to be okay with my post-baby stretch marks. Also, there was probably nothing scarier for me than this:

Posing in glitter-encrusted dental floss;

Sprayed like an Oompa Loompa fell into the chocolate river;

In six-inch plastic heels;

On a stage;

In a room of well over 100 people.

Given my klutzy nature, the risk of falling and becoming a viral YouTube sensation was extreme. If I were betting on it, I would have bet on that happening.

"Okay, so tell me about the mental battles, then, before you get to the acupuncture. It sounds like a story here. Do you want a drink or something?"

"I'll have a champagne, thanks." I sighed and started telling the story. "Well, I figured there were three mental battles. Battle #1: Being hangry and wanting to do bad things to Nutella."

"Okay, I get the hangry, go on. What happened?"

"Well, I tried really hard to be introspective and observe what my brain was doing when I went from eating relatively healthy to eating very disciplined, weighing chicken, broccoli and brown rice, and smashing egg whites like M&M's.

"The focus here is *tried*. I got hangry at my kids as my carbs were depleted, and my energy was smashed. They were just behaving like normal kids, leaving normal mess, and I turned into a bit of a bitch mother – or momster – while my body tried to adjust. Mostly because I was trying to make sure that my kids were still eating normally, and still got their little treats (which for me were temptations). Little treats like Nutella… mmm, Nutella.

"It's a good indication of the mental battle you are facing when you find yourself staring at a jar of Nutella that you bought for your kids, trying not to tongue kiss the last bits inside the jar."

Baker laughed. "Well, that's quite a visual. You're funny!"

I felt my cheeks go red and thanked God that I was wearing

foundation, something I normally don't do. I was hoping my blushing was not showing. I couldn't believe he was still sitting there talking to me. *Why?*

"It's the truth! That's about how passionate I can get with a jar of Nutella when all I have been eating is four egg whites, 50 grams of steamed chicken and 100 grams of steamed broccoli for breakfast, lunch and dinner. Yep – you've got that visual. It's pretty disturbing. Satisfying, but disturbing. I wanted to understand what it took to prepare for a bikini competition. It did make me appreciate the organisation, the focus and the discipline that these athletes have to get to stage. They work super-hard. Mentally and physically."

"So, how'd you do on the mental one?"

"Well, I like to think I'm quite strong mentally, so I did okay. The next battle was a little more tricky: wearing six-inch perspex stripper heels."

Baker looked shocked, and blushed at the mention of stripper heels. *Guess he's a conservative person,* I thought. I tried to explain myself in a flurry of embarrassment.

"What I mean is, for a bikini comp, well, the only way I can describe these shoes is like stripper heels. Well, at least that's what they look like online. You wear them to make your legs look extra-long. I actually thought I'd be okay at the walking and posing part. Not so much."

Baker leaned in, and whispered in my ear... "Why did you think it would be easy, is that something you have done before? You know, um, ah, 'stripping'?"

"NO!"

The rock god squad turned its attention towards us. My denial was quite shouty.

Lowering my voice, "No. I have not done that before. I did a brief catwalk stint, though, before I turned 18. I thought it would be a good idea to try my hand at learning how to walk like a model. It was more about improving my actual walking abilities and my posture, as I was quite self-conscious of my height. I used to hunch over during high school. There were not a lot of tall boys around.

"Dad was mortified, my mum delighted. But it was a career that never took off. I did get the turns down pat, though, so having that little background, I thought I'd be okay with, 'Hey, let's walk in stripper heels and strike a pose and suck everything in and flex your booty' front. I was not okay on that front. At. All."

He didn't seem to understand. "Why not?"

"Well, maybe because a good 20 years had passed since I'd done any type of walking and posing. Maybe because things had stiffened up on the body front over time. Maybe it's because I had stiffened up on trying new things. Either way, awkward."

"So, what'd you do?"

"Well, I went to see a posing coach in the outer suburbs. I swear if I'd driven any further I would have ended up in Adelaide.

"The instructions were: wear Lycra, bring your stripper heels and have a sports bra on so we can see your body. It was sooo daunting. When someone critiques your body that you personally think is looking okay aside from your stomach, and they tell you you're 'probably not going to be stage ready', it's quite confronting. Not in a bad way, just the way that is in that sport and industry. Nothing was said out of meanness – it's just feedback. Confronting feedback, but still feedback. 'Your legs look good, your mid-section needs work, your shoulders are shaping up nicely – but you can't walk and pose yet; you are stiffer than my grandfather's five o'clock scotch."

"That's pretty harsh," he said.

I couldn't believe he was still sitting here listening to my story. Maybe he liked hearing tales of dorkiness, I don't know.

"Ummm, if you want to go chat to someone else, it's fine. It's a dumb story anyway."

"No, you still need to tell me what happened with the acupuncture person. I need to know. It might help. So keep going."

Gosh, this conversation would have been easier if he were gay, a douchebag, rude, or all of the above. But he was just a nice guy. A super-hot, positive, nice guy. Damn it. I could feel my awkwardness spilling over, but I tried to continue.

"Well… their feedback wasn't harsh – not really. If you have seen baby giraffes on any *Animal Planet* documentaries, and you imagine putting a pair of six-inch plastic stilettos on the baby giraffe and dressing the baby giraffe – let's call her Georgia – in Lycra, that would be me. I could hardly walk in the fucking things! Trying to walk with grace and flex muscles is a bit of a stretch. It's way harder than it looks.

"You'd be surprised how much of a workout walking in heels and posing actually is. It's also hard when you are trying to remember foot placement, step the left leg, pop the right hip, bring the right leg over, do some little hand gesture thing, twist your torso and smile, SMILE, damn it! Plus look like you are enjoying this, and you don't need a colonic. Oh, God!

"The other advice I got was, 'The stage will always be there, so it's better to be ready, and if you are doing all this work, then you should do it to win'. Fair point, really. If we are doing anything, why would we just half-arse it?"

"Okay, that is two battles. What is the third one?" he pressed.

"Battle #3: Stay injury free. This is where I ran into trouble, and why I'm reluctant to see an acupuncture person again. I'm surprised I'm not blacklisted on some secret Acupuncture Society Facebook page or something."

"Did you twist your ankle in the heels or something?"

"Not quite... Each week I kept up my training with Becs – weight training five times a week, cardio six times a week, eating all the flipping chicken and broccoli. Making sure I stretched and went for massages. Tick, tick, tick. I thought I was doing great. Little muscle soreness, but I could train and run and put kindy kids to bed single-handedly without straining a hammie. All going great. Then I got taken out by a super-short man."

"What, like a sniper? Or a date?"

"Not on a date or anything nice. Although it did involve night-time. And the man was in my bedroom. And he took me down – literally brought me to my knees. Not romantically, though. More in the style of how bad guys get taken down by a booby trap in an action movie, so kinda sniper-style."

"What, like a crime? Were you hurt? I hate bad guys!"

I watched his facial expressions as he was drawn into my story. I was surprised at how easy it was to chat to him, even though I felt like I should not be talking to him at all, not on this very glammed-up table. But then again, Becs liked my stories – there was always laughing in her gym.

"Nah... good guy, actually. I got up in the middle of the night to let my dog outside. Anyway, I didn't turn on lights or anything, and as I got up and walked two steps from my bed, I stood on a piece of stupid Lego. A Lego man, to be exact. The tiny green ninja – I think his name is Lloyd. Were you a Lego lover?"

"Hell, yeah! I've still got the Death Star from *Star Wars*."

"Oh, well I've got Lego love-hate. I love it for kids. It would be fair to say there's a few containers of Lego in my house. I never owned any growing up as it was super-expensive, so I've probably been compensating for stuff I wanted. But maybe it was because my mum knew something that I've learned."

"Oh?"

"It goes everywhere. My dog likes to steal it as part of a game and then chew a critical piece up and your master build of a tropical island complete with jet skis and monkeys for small plastic people is over. What's more, either a kid or the dog will randomly dump it on my bedroom floor. So, for whatever reason, I hadn't bothered to pick it up. I might have been having a day where kid crap everywhere versus me cleaning saw the kid crap win. I probably prioritised other stuff. Like weighing the chicken, or working and earning money and putting a roof over our heads. Anyway, I stood on the stupid piece of Lego, and it damaged a part of my foot, trapping the Baxter nerve. Baxter nerve entrapment is painful. Do you know about that?"

"Well, I know about it from a physiological point of view, but I've never done an injury myself."

"Every time I took a step, it hurt like a mother. Didn't matter whether I was walking on my tippy toes, in flats, or in runners – it really hurt and would send shooting pain through my foot and my Achilles. It put a stop to my cardio training. I went back for one more posing class just to see if competing was still possible. I tried walking in the stripper heels, only to find that the pain was too great."

"Oh, no! After all that chicken weighing and all that broccoli, what did you do?"

"Honestly? I said thanks, I'll see you some other time, got in the car, drove to the nearest milk bar and smashed a bucket of hot chips – even the dodgy, burnt-on-the-corner chips. After all the hot chips, I called and booked in to see a podiatrist to get the injury sorted."

"But podiatrists do feet – how does acupuncture fit?"

"I know, right! I wasn't expecting needles from a podiatrist. I think deep down this podiatry chick probably had a side hobby of voodoo dolls and liked sticking pins in things, so had figured out a way to incorporate that passion with feet. I mean, how do you do it?"

"I don't really think about it. The needles aren't going in me! What happened, though? Where did they put the needles, because foot needles are pretty painful."

"Damn straight foot needles are painful. Turns out Lego is loved by podiatrists – they see a lot of parents with Lego injuries. So there I am. In the podiatrist's office – let's call her June – foot outstretched. She asks if I've had acupuncture before. It went like this…"

Baker looked at me, wondering what I was about to do.

I cleared my voice and started my best posh fancy voice. Just like what June sounded like.

"'Based on my assessment, I'd like to do some dry needling. Have you had acupuncture before?'

"And I tell June, 'Yeah, I'm pretty good with pain. I had it a few times when I lived in Queensland from some old Chinese dude. I don't find that acupuncture hurts too much.'

"So June says (once again my silly voice came on, which was getting some laughs from Bakes), 'Okay, well you will probably need three or four sessions, given the muscles in your foot have spasmed around the Baxter nerve, and we need to release the muscles, then strap your foot.'

"I say, 'That's cool', and June says, 'Well, this might hurt.'

"Knowing I have a pretty good pain threshold, I say, 'I'm sweet, June! I don't even take Panadol.'"

Baker is hooked. "And…?"

"I sit up on the massage table with my jeans rolled up, while June asks me to wriggle forward. She gets her needles out of her desk drawer and sits them to the side of my foot.

"They look a bit bigger than the acupuncture needles I have seen before. As in thicker and more painful. Maybe I just remembered them thinner.

"The first needle goes in. I swear on the inside, like a group of sailors having a cussing competition. I'm thinking to myself, *I'm screwed if there are more needles!*"

"Sounds like June might have a secret voodoo doll hobby after all."

"Well, I did wonder if she had a drawer full of pin cushions shaped like her patients' feet."

"Bet she's got Lego traps, too," Baker joked.

"Haha. Anyway, I let out an audible 'aaaaaaahhhhhh', probably a little too high-pitched. More like a scream. I say to June: 'June, how many needles are you going to put in?'

"And June says, 'Oh, just a few more, and then I'm just going to tap them ever so slightly.'"

"Do you always do funny voices?"

"Only when I'm really nervous. Anyway... I look at June with a face that looks like I just ate the cupcake my daughter made where she got the sugar and baking soda mixed up and it tasted like arse so much that my face could not hide it. So I breathe out, and try to talk myself into being okay."

"Are you?"

"Nope. Not at all... wait for it! The second needle goes in; this time, I let out an audible 'Fuuuuuuuck! Shit, sorry for swearing! But fuck!' June looks at me and I'm sure she is evil-smiling.

"Then comes the third needle, and my ninja reflexes kick in..."

"You must have got them from standing on Lloyd the green Lego ninja."

Baker's eyes sparkled. *I could just stare at this face... Oh no! What's happening?* I thought desperately.

"Quite possibly. Anyway, my other leg reacts, swings around and clean sweeps June off her little swivel chair onto the floor.

"So I say, 'Shit. June! June! Are you okay?'"

"Was she okay?"

"Well, June was on the floor, a little dishevelled. I'm thinking, *Oh, crap. I can't actually put my foot down as I've still got needles stuck in there*, right?"

"So then what?" Baker inched closer to me. Our chairs were facing each other; I was unaware of the other table chat going on around us.

"Well, I have no choice but to call out loudly for help. Anyway, the receptionist comes in to see what all the commotion is about, and helps June back up."

"Ah, poor evil June! Was she okay?"

"Yeah. She recovered, but talk about embarrassing. She's not done yet, though. The last needle goes in and it hurts just as much as the others. It is excruciating pain. Not the acupuncture needles I remember from my old North Queensland Chinese medicine man days."

"Did you go back? I normally treat people a few times."

"Yeah. Three more times. Humiliating. Which is why it's safer if acupuncturists are not left alone in a room with me. They might get hurt."

"Well, that's quite a story. Hey, do you know how to put this 3D puzzle together? It has no sharp edges, so we should be safe."

My self-confidence was so busy dorking out because conversation with this guy was so easy. *He's funny, positive, charming, probably has inner-dork tendencies like me. It's really easy to like him. I can't believe that someone who is super-hot is actually talking to me – still.*

The event progressed, and it turned out that the table was full of not just beautiful-on-the-outside people but beautiful-on-the-inside people. It was an eclectic mix of mostly business owners, some in the health industry, some in beauty, and some – like me – in the business of supporting businesses.

What we all had in common, though, was that nine out of 10 of us on the table had been affected by mental health, hence coming to support the charity event.

Despite the night being fun, I managed to say my goodbyes and slip away, impressed by this beautiful man. I made a few new contacts and friends to catch up with. I told myself that someone like Baker would not be interested in someone like me anyway. Plus, I was busy with the business, the kids, the house… Life was simple and uncomplicated.

"Jo, I had forgotten the energy of this man. I had not seen him since last December. I had completely forgotten the impression he made, and I was very wary of going to see him, since the last time I had any needles shoved in to sort things out, it was in my foot. It was bad enough roundhousing a little old lady. And I was wearing clothes then. It would be way worse if I kicked a hot guy in my mum undies."

"Okay, so we know that the mum undies happened. You need to go and buy some hot new undies. You'll feel better. Big W have some nice ones. Go get some."

"I'll put it on the list."

"Just do it for you. It will make you feel better. Are nice undies and bras that low on the priority list just because they are hidden?"

"Perhaps they should be like our thoughts... Choose ones that make you feel good and see what happens. Just because they can't be seen, doesn't mean they don't matter. Promise I'll put it on the list."

I'm sad to admit, the bras haven't even been replaced for God knows how long. They are worn. One is missing an underwire. The undie drawer is just sad. I really should do something about it.

I continue, "The Monday after pole fitness, I haven't given a thought to the state of ANYTHING unseen. Socks. Undies. Memories. Nada. Doesn't hit the radar."

"Sock bucket situation?" Jo asks.

"Yes. Total sock bucket situation."

She starts to laugh.

If the tops of my socks are the same make and same colour, I take that as a win. Even now, if you were to meet me in person, there is a high chance that my socks don't fully match. I don't care, really. I gave up ticking the matching-socks-equals-a-successful-fully-functioning-adult box after amassing what is now known as 'the sock bucket'.

Yes, I have a bucket – about 20 litres. It's a beautiful metal bucket with a wooden handle, powder-coated in an apricot colour. It sits in my laundry. One day after getting super-shitty about mismatched socks in the laundry that needed to be folded, I caved. I think the odd socks either happen because washing machines eat them, or the kids come back from their dad's house with odd socks (co-parenting first-world problems), or I find one of my son's socks tied to the dog's collar and the other one, well, who the heck knows where that one is – probably in the freezer or on the trampoline. I started the sock bucket in the hope that I'd be able to eventually find matches and get those socks back together. That didn't happen. The sock bucket has turned into a game of 'get two socks and if they are the same colour at the top, wear them'.

"Despite my being dressed all profesh for a coaching appointment, I forget in the morning that I'll be disrobing and ending up on the table. I think I have one blue one on and one white one. They have white tops, are inside ankle boots, and really, I'm not thinking about anyone seeing my socks."

Jo comes closer to the phone again. "So tell me what happened. And keep the code name. I like it. Makes it fun."

I'd driven to Baker's studio, in excruciating pain. It was the sciatica thing. I'd started tearing up in the car, just from the pain. Vulnerability – even physical vulnerability – is something that I am not so great at showing. I mean, I refused to scream during the birth of my son because I didn't want to wake up sleeping three-year-old Abby who was parked in the stroller in the corner of the delivery room.

Driving gave me time to think about strength, and how strength also comes in softness. Softness I might have stuffed away after all the loss and all the hurdles the universe had placed on my running track.

Could I teach my kids softness? Surely I needed to teach them that falling down was okay. Emotions are okay. Living life and finding joy are okay. That being some weird-arse superwoman is not all it's cracked up to be, and that she has a time and a place to wear the cape, and a time and a place to take it off, stuff it in the wardrobe and just be her naked-souled self.

I worked to switch my brain off from overthinking things. Mostly because when I get into thinking mode in the car, I miss what Sat Nav James is talking to me about in his British accent and drive straight past my exit. Huh – I've done that a few times before. Singing along to music helps. Not that day, though. Nothing was really distracting me from the pain, or the anxiety about once again being face down on a table. Not even my hope that a few well-placed acupuncture needles would release whatever muscles were spasming around my sciatic nerve and give me some relief.

Baker works from a studio out the back of a house. He rents a granny flat, close to the beach. Minimal. Clutter free.

I'd rocked up and hobbled around the back, not quite sure where to go, waiting for some random dog or something to come attack me at any moment.

Out walked Hot Hands. I'd forgotten just how hot he looked. My stomach flipped and my knees went weak as my brain went into overdrive about all my flaws, the state of the mismatched mum undies, the odd socks, where I was going to look (thankfully, through a massage table hole). Whether I'd be able to hold any form of conversation for an hour, or if it would be more of an awkward silence interspersed with anatomical questions about the state of my sciatica and how I did the injury.

"Hey, Belle! You poor thing – how'd you go driving here?"

Holding back the tears, "Well, it didn't tickle, I can tell you that much."

"What did you do to yourself?"

"Ummm, I kinda went pole dancing with my friend Lauren and fell off the pole."

Embarrassing

Reminded again of how hot he was, I wished I could turn into a whitewash chameleon and blend in with the studio walls. I wished I'd worn matching socks, too.

All my nerd insecurities came flooding back, raining down on my confidence so heavily my brain needed to build a freakin' ark! *Oh my God, oh my God. Why did you not remember how hot he was? Could your undie selection be any worse? No, wait, maybe it's not so bad. How old are they anyway? Oh, shit! They are the black and white ones you've had since Abby was born. Oh, no! It will be okay... there will be a towel over the area anyway. How are you going to talk to anyone THAT hot? Maybe he will be the type of acupuncturist who plays some kind of hippy rain music and doesn't speak. Least you won't have to look the guy in the eye. Okay, Belle, pull yourself together.*

Into the studio we went. We had a quick chat about the issue with my sciatic nerve before I went facedown on the table. Thank God it wasn't a front-of-body injury. No eye contact. That's good. I thought if I made eye contact with him I might involuntarily giggle like an idiot and say something random that makes no sense at all, like I have a crush on Toyota FJ Cruisers. Then, because of his hotness, I would combust into flames on the massage table and leave him mentally scarred.

Talk about awkward. I stared through the tiny breakfast-bowl-sized hole at my hands, which were placed on the blue hand rest thing in front of me, while Baker felt down the backs of my legs and around my lower back and the side of my hips before working out where the needles were going to go.

Internally, I searched for some type of chit-chat to get into. Given we were near the beach, and surfing is on my list of things to do, I asked, "So, um... do you surf?" God, I may as well have asked if he came here often.

"Yeah, I like to get out, you?"

"It's next on my list of things to do with Lauren."

"List – what list?"

"Oh, I have this year-of-being-brave list thing, and my friend Lauren is doing some of the stuff with me. So surfing is on the list. She's scared of wetsuits – claustrophobic. You scared of sharks or wetsuits?"

"Well, now that you've mentioned them, I'm scared of everything!"

"Wetsuits and sharks?"

"No – just sharks."

"I know that if I had to choose between a shark and a crocodile in a fight, I'd choose a shark."

"I reckon I could take on a croc."

"Really?"

"Yep. I'd totally win in a wrestle with a croc and then turn him into a belt."

"Well, you take on the crocs, and I'll take on the sharks. Crocs scare me. I learnt to waterski in North Queensland in the rivers with my older sister. She didn't tell me until after that there were crocs in the river we were on. Crocs stuff you in a hidey hole for snacking on later. Do you still think you would win?"

"Yep. One hundred percent. Sharks are super-fast. Crocs are slow."

"But I think sharks biting people are more a case of, 'Whoops, my bad, thought you were a seal in that wetsuit.'"

"Needle coming… just relax – breathe out."

His hand rested on the top of my shoulder, before moving and placing the first needle in.

"Eeek."

"I've only got to see a shadow in the water, though, and I Fred Flintstone on out of there," he said, ignoring my undignified sound.

"Ha! I get that. When I was little, I used to be scared of my own shadow down at the beach. I thought it was actually a patch of seaweed, and that blue swimmer crabs were going to come and bite me."

"You seem like a pretty capable lady, though. If we went somewhere and there were muggers, I reckon you'd take them on."

"Um, not so sure about that... So you're saying I'd be left to fend for myself?"

"Nah, I'd just be hiding behind you. Are you scared of anything?"

"Yep. Frogs. Terrified."

"What? Little green froggies? Why?"

"Oh, that is a whole other story for another day. But overcoming them is on my list for being brave this year."

As the acupuncture wrapped up, he gave me some stretches to do, and that was that.

I'd left reminded of a few things and thinking maybe, just maybe, I should start putting myself back out there again. You know, being vulnerable and working towards what was, for me, the ultimate act of bravery – facing those fears of rejection.

Not with Bakes, though – he's like an advanced barrel wave surf. I'm still at boogie-board-in-the-whitewash level.

* * *

"So, Jo, the conversation was easy. He is still the positive, happy guy that I met last year at the Gatsby event. I'm not sure about the 'being his body shield' thing. I don't want to be seen as the masculine person. It kinda felt like a backhanded compliment…"

"Maybe not intended that way."

"But when he hugged me as I left. Oh. My. God."

"What – what could you tell?"

"You know when you see, like, hard bodies. Like, buff, could-be-in-an-action-movie bodies. Like The Rock? But not as tall as The Rock. It was like… butter. Melting into butter. No, wait…. I'd be the butter. He'd be the – oh, who cares what he'd be. Hot bread. Arms that feel like they could save you – that, or push you in front of a mugger as a shield. And his chest. I reckon he has a 12-pack, not just a six-pack. That man is not eating doughnuts all day long, I can tell you that. He could be my thank you and good night, if you get what I mean." I wink at her.

"Bet you're regretting your undie choice," Jo says.

"Um, nope. If I have to go back, I'm keeping my crush cards close to my chest, thanks!"

"And that is brave how?"

"Give me time – it's only February. Waaay down the list. I have to talk to the kids about dating first."

"I think you should go back. Oh, and what's happening with the workshops? It's been five years since we met, right? Tell me later. I've just realised the time! Shit! Claire! We need to…"

Her voice trails off as she hangs up on FaceTime, and once again, my friend disappears back into her world of wild and free foraging, and I disappear back into suburbia and business planning.

3

MARCH

*J*o and I met in the pilot program I ran five years ago. The pilot program that saw me take all my corporate-pants knowledge and help mums in business. The pilot program that fuelled my purpose in creating options outside the traditional nine-to-five.

Five years ago, jammed with the 20 other women I was supporting into the Halls Head rec room, with uneven tables, a tiny TV for presenting, and me wondering if I had what it takes. Five years ago, while Jo breastfed a six-week-old baby and utilised the creche so she could do the Mumpreneur program with me and a heap of other women.

I mean, shit. There I was imparting my business knowledge, and I had someone like Jo in the room who had a degree in entrepreneurship. Talk about wondering if you have what it takes, or if you might be full of shit. *Hello, self-doubt. I'll just park you and get on with it.*

She'd wandered up to me in the car park while I was packing resources into the back of my soon-to-die blue Subaru that had made its way over from Melbourne. At that time, I still hadn't embraced living in the west. I hadn't changed my license plates over. I wasn't sure if I could do the slower pace of WA after my Melbourne life. But I wanted to design it and do it different, and help other women do the same. Nine-to-five is so broken.

"I could see your password!" That was her opening line.

I'd stared at her, bemused with her honesty. "Oh, right. Thanks. Do you want a hand with anything?"

"No. I just thought you should know that when you are presenting and you have to put your password into your iPad, I can see it on the TV screen. Not that I'm going to mug you or anything, but I thought you should know. It's kinda like flashing your electronic knickers accidentally, so I thought you might want to know that I could see your knickers. I mean your iPad knickers."

We had become fast friends. She'd told me that my 'stuff' was good. By which she meant the workshop. That she had a degree in entrepreneurship, but this was really, really good.

And really, I had started those programs for a few reasons. Here I was back in the west, with zero network, zero friends. Working at creating a life so I could be there for my kids, and use my biz brain for good, and take all that knowledge of how to do more with less from my corporate days of watching restructuring of offers happen and use it to help get mums up and running in business.

Sometimes when you are thinking of people, they just magically ring you. Sometimes you are still in bed, because it's 5 am where you live, and it's 8 am where they live.

"Hey," Jo says, "so I was thinking about our chat from last week. Remind me how you ended up doing these programs anyway? I'm just driving – I've dropped Claire off to school and I might hit the forest and the dead patch."

I dive into the story with her.

I had been sold the 'you can do anything, be anything, have it all' message that came with being a teenage girl in the late '80s, early '90s. It was a message that I didn't fully understand, and one that lead to my exit from the corporate world – like other mums – as I realised that the nine-to-five model didn't work for us.

A well-meaning career guidance counsellor, Mrs Rodgers, had changed the course of my happy little free-spirited life plan.

I'd wandered in to sit with her in her small office. My high school was not really well regarded in the state. When a kid gets expelled for composing drug deals in French class and later goes on to commit terrible crimes at 14, it would be fair to say it was on the rougher side of the tracks.

At that stage, I wanted to be a flight attendant. I loved languages, travel, and it was a way out. Except apparently that dream was not the right one.

"Why be a flight attendant when you could be the pilot?"

Guess why, Mrs Rodgers. Go on, guess.

Because I loved French and fucking hated physics. Pilots need physics, and apart from laws of gravity and a few other rando things, I distinctly remember thinking poking out my eyes with Bunsen burners would have been more enjoyable. I mean, what the fuck was wrong with being a flight attendant?

Unfortunately, I didn't know back then that I should have said thanks, but no thanks, studied French some more and stuck to my flight attendant-slash-become-a-writer plan.

I'd grown up knowing what it was like to not have money. To want to join the Bluebirds under-8s netball team or do gymnastics or roller-skating lessons but be told, "No, if your sister can't do it, you can't either," which was really code for 'we have no money'. And I really didn't want to be poor. I wanted opportunities.

So with those thoughts in mind, I decided that perhaps Mrs Rodgers was right. That my goal wasn't good enough.

I took that message and owned it, not realising the versions of success I was buying into.

I never made it to uni straight out of high school, even though I got an offer. This was on account of Mum's depression and her sitting my placement offer on top of the fridge, which I discovered months later.

I got a normal job that over time turned into three jobs – one full-time in a buying office, one part-time as a door bitch for a coat room at a nightclub, and one as a waitress helping with catering events. All so I could save up and get the hell out of the west.

As the career chase went on and the adventures got funded, those dreams slipped and I found myself early-thirties, pregnant with my first child, quietly wondering how I would do the magical 'it all'. When I hit the due date, and the baby was still on the inside like some prized mega watermelon, I decided that I would do what I do best. I'd—

"Hello??? Jo??"

Damn phone network. With no more Jo and the quiet of the morning before the kids wake up, I have time to think about my older sister, Witchy. I'd officially outlive her this year. She was 43. The anniversary of her death had passed. Her birthday was around the corner…

I start reflecting back on the conversation with Witchy.

It was official. The 2008 due date for baby number one was here. Abby – my daughter formerly known as 'the bump' – was running late. I was sitting in the needs-renovating financial-pressure-cooker cottage eight kilometres from the centre of Melbourne, in the tiny kitchen with the oversized table – 'living the dream'.

I had become super-organised. I was even going to attend a work planning day because I was all nested out and bored.

Super-organised for me meant I had read all the books, looked at the meaning of all the names, and decided to pre-type a text to announce the arrival of little miss Abby. I didn't trust her dad to do a good enough job text-wise when we were in the delivery room. Sorry.

Sitting in my kitchen, wedged between the wall heater that didn't work and the eight-seater table that was way too big for the space, I had my trusty mobile phone (I think it was a Sony flip phone – I hadn't gone team iPhone as yet). I painstakingly sat there and typed up what I thought would be a good text, in preparation for the arrival.

I mean, it was my due date, so surely this baby was going to vacate her residence any time now. Like, any.

The text read like this.

To: ALL ADDRESS BOOK

Content: We are pleased to announce the arrival of Baby Bump aka *accidentally hit send instead of save to draft*.

Shit. How do I recall a text message?

Then my phone started going OFF.

"Congratulations! Did you have a boy or a girl?"

"That's awesome news."

"How big, are you okay?"

"What hospital are you at?"

"DID IT END UP BEING TWINS – COZ YOU WERE HUUUGE."

"Um, Bee, Mum just called and is upset that she got a group text – why haven't you called me to say that you are at the hospital? Did we have a boy or a girl?"

As my phone started pinging non-stop, my beautiful big sister rang me.

"Congratulations, baby sis!"

There was silence on the phone.

"Umm, I'm still pregnant."

"But what about the text?"

"I was trying to be organised and I accidentally sent a text. To EVERYONE."

Witchy started laughing hysterically.

"You dickhead. Trust you to do something like that."

Yep. Trust me.

I pictured her face. I pictured her sitting outside on her verandah. I smiled at the time I had spent with her and her kids in my early twenties after Mum died. It was nice to visualise her happy face in the corner of my mind. High forehead. Sandy blonde fringe sweeping to one side. Her head cocked to one side so she could listen with intensity to what you were saying, given her deafness in one ear. Probably not wearing shoes, but shorts and a T-shirt, with her feet tucked up in a squat position on a chair while she waited for her coffee to cool a little.

Even though she was excited about me becoming a mum, I sensed something was off. I was excited to have her to talk to about any mother-y type stuff, considering, you know, my own parental shortage.

We joked as she thought that I would never have kids. To be honest, I didn't know if I would or not – babies were something that I never got particularly clucky over.

"I have something to tell you," Witchy uttered. "And I'm really sorry about the timing, because I know that you are having a baby, like, any day."

I knew it wasn't good. My big sister was the QUEEN of self-sacrifice. Terrible habit.

She'd had health issues for quite some time, and no amount of me nagging her over the years since we'd been hanging out in Queensland during my twenties would get her to go and sort it out fully.

Witchy had put it down to painful periods from having butterfly clips attached to her fallopian tubes and going through ectopic pregnancies multiple times. Except things had taken a wrong turn.

She didn't even have to say the words. The silence on the phone and her breathing was telling.

So I said the words.

"You have cancer, don't you, Witchy?"

Silence again. But not the awkward 'haha, you dickhead' silence. It was the other silence. The get-ready-to-batten-down-the-emotional-hatches silence. Get ready for a storm. Get ready to stop your eyeballs from emoting while you work this one out.

I heard her start to cry. Her breath sucked back into her lungs over the phone, as her sob came out.

Not exactly the start to being a first-time mum I was hoping for.

"Yes," she said. "I'm sorry... I'm so sorry, baby. You can't tell the others yet, because they will just freak out and come up straight away, and I need to get my head around this."

"Okay, I promise."

Here I was, massively fucking pregnant, with a half-a-million-dollar mortgage, and my knowledge bank to motherhood, my rock – MY person – was dying. When we met with Mum's death, our sisterhood was really born. Warrior sisters.

She was an ally in death, in grief and in life. She was someone who could crack a joke amidst the darkness and shine a light on the absurdity of life. Someone filled with light despite personal battles and losses. We didn't know of each other's battle scars, but we sure as hell saw each other's light.

She was my person. And she had just blindsided me. But I knew she would fight. I mean, she had five kids. Plus, she had me.

As I listened to her tears on the phone, I heard a thunderstorm start to roll in. It sounded like the ones we had watched during the sugar cane harvest season together, sharing stories and Winnie Blues. She got me. In all ways, she got me. Jokes. Perseverance. Secrets. Stubbornness. Stubbornness to prove that you had, in fact, earned your battle scars. Earned your seat to tell stories out under those thunderstorms. Stories of your own wars, your own losses. Stories of how forgiveness really was the only medicine that helped heal battle scars.

She was the sister in the family that everyone loved, even when sibling battles were afoot.

The big sister.

Fuck. Fucking fucking fuck of a fuck you stupid fucking cancer.

I mean, come on, universe, God – how many people do you have to take? What lesson am I not learning? How strong do I need to be?

I tried to compose myself and not let my anger spill out while I tried to be the rock. I questioned her on what it was, keeping my game face on. I have a great game face – it's really good at looking like a duck on a pond when, beneath the surface, everything is swirling around in muddy waters, working to keep the upper layer composed. Stupid fucking duck pond.

"Metastatic melanoma. You know the ad where it looks like a spider, and it travels through your body and latches on to other parts of your body? Well, it's that one."

"But you don't even sunbake?"

"No – it's residual from a skin cancer that was removed 10 years ago on my stomach."

"So, how serious is it? Can they do chemo?"

"Yes – I'm starting chemo tomorrow. Success depends on where it has spread to."

I knew my big sister. She wouldn't just give in like my dad had, or check out like our mum – although Mum was different.

"I love you, let me know what I can do and when you want me to come up."

"Okay, babe. I will. Take care – I love you, too."

I stared at my phone, unable to respond with a group text to tell everyone that I was in fact still very pregnant.

And I stayed pregnant for a good eight days past the due date, not realising what cataclysmic shit storm was about to unfold within the next five months.

In early 2009, I could feel them. Ticking time bombs. Boob bombs.

Breastfeeding bombs that were about the only thing that had remained super-organised in my new mum life. Breastfeeding boob bombs that were about to start spraying on the inside of my shirt like a pin had been placed in a water balloon, and they had a countdown timer. Breast pads would not stand a chance. And I was wearing a white shirt. What. The Fudgemonkey. Was I thinking?

I sat there in the user acceptance testing meeting for new software changes. Two women in the room, one of them me. The rest men. The meeting that was to finish at 5 pm, but looked like it was going to run over.

On one hand, I had a five-month-old baby about six kilometres away who would be waiting, expecting her mum to be rocking up any moment for her feed. Mum fail, activate. On the other hand, I had a meeting that I was going to have to bail on or start my own lactation wet T-shirt competition, where I'd be the winner. Previously awesome employee fail, activate.

There had to be a better way. A way to lighten the 'you can do all the things' load. I was dreaming of it, as I listened to Gordo talk through processes and next steps. I'd spoken with Jacqueline – a coach who would turn into one of my closest friends – about my magical escape plan, and the birth of workingmumcoach.com, my first side hustle where I'd help working mums negotiate better work flexibility.

In split seconds, I started to feel the boobs go off like a time bomb. No green wire or red wire. Just baby-needs-a-feed wire.

The load was not just that of a working mum. My older sister, my person, was dying. She was in my thoughts daily.

Yet there I was, having returned to work full-time when my daughter was three-and-a-half months old. Not my dream. But have a half-a-million-dollar mortgage with an eight percent interest rate and an obliterated 'rainy day/take time out to be a mum' share portfolio thanks to the GFC, and thou shalt return to work, thou shalt not get back into the skinny jeans, and thou shalt try to be super-organised, and bond where possible.

I had been determined to breastfeed my now-five-month-old daughter – I really wanted that bond with her, which in all honesty did not come easy.

Gordo, who was a little old-school but really did try to be progressive in supporting women at work, started to prattle on some more.

There were roughly 20 of us in the room, and it was 4:59 pm, and ticking. I was ready for things to wrap up, and figured I could last roughly another eight minutes before I started running into trouble. The afternoon feed had been starting at around 5:10 pm.

My boobs had developed this uncanny ability to tell the time. I mean, you could set a clock by those puppies. It really became a case of 'at the third stroke, breast milk will come spraying out of your tits all over your child and anything else in range if she is not attached.' Ticking timeboobs.

As Gordo kept talking, and I internally tried to balance being a good, attentive worker and getting to a baby that needed feeding, a biological decision was being made for me… Get the fuck out of the meeting before your top ends up soaked in front of about 17 blokes.

"Gordo, I'm sorry to interrupt, but I've got to go."

"Can you wait five more minutes, Belle?"

The internal ugh went off as I felt the judgement about having to leave, so I made a call…

"Under normal circumstances I'd be able to wait 20 more minutes, but there is a five-month-old baby who is expecting me for a meeting."

Gordo stared at me blankly.

"I don't get it – surely the baby can wait a couple more minutes," he said.

Donna, who was sitting next to me, whispered in my ear, "Just say it – they need to learn."

I started packing up my things as I felt the left boob – the side she fed from first – start to go, signalling 5:10 pm. Shit…

I tried to summon as much inner calm as I could, one, in the hope that I'd somehow magically delay the spray that had started inside my top, and two, that I wouldn't screw up the job and the enormous amount of financial pressure I felt.

"Gordo. My baby is not on solids – I'm breastfeeding, and if I stand here talking for another five minutes, my boobs are literally going to explode and breast pads can only do so much. I'd rather not have my first foray into wet T-shirts happen at work in a meeting with 17 blokes around the table. Now if you'll excuse me, I have got to go before things get weird."

As my outburst – I prefer to think of it as taking a stand for working mums – unfolded, I saw all the blokes in the room shuffle papers and try to look at the motivational posters of rock climbers, people hanging from cliffs, and the one about customers being an ocean or some shit for either guidance or just distraction in case they accidentally saw my left boob exploding. Poor blokes.

As I raced out the door, I called out that I'd get the notes from Donna, and sorry about the situation, but it was biological.

Perhaps as I struggled with the juggle – or if I am being nice about it, perhaps as I did my best with what I knew of navigating working parenthood – I somehow forgot to actually ask for help.

It became a case of, 'Hey, is Belle waving, or drowning?' and me more than likely telling people that I was waving, when in actual fact I was drowning.

As I raced from the office to the daycare, and did my best to balance it all, the outside smiled while the inside just disappeared. As this disappearance happened, it was unfortunate for my little Abby. She was about to unknowingly see her adventurous, 'take no prisoners' mum disappear under the weight of everything.

I picked her up, breastfed her, and made my way home through inner-city Melbourne traffic to our wonky old house that needed renovating.

Bath.

Dinner.

Her dad went to soccer training.

I pulled out the laptop and worked. Nine-to-five my engorged mammaries! More like nine-to-nine.

Bed.

Next day, 5 am. Wake up and repeat.

Except the next day things went down. Really down.

I'd been at an offsite strategy meeting when the call came. Right before I had to present.

I'd had calls before about family members dying.

When my mum died, it felt like I had opened the door only to be punched with the full force of the universe in the chest. I've not been physically punched before – with the exception of a boxing class – but I imagine when the wind is fully taken out of you from a punch, it feels like that day did.

The punch that you don't see coming. Blindsided.

With my dad when I was 29 – I know, you should see my completed family history at the doctors. I try to put a smiley face on the bottom, as I can just see them going, "Oh, lady, you are genetically screwed". It was slow motion. I'd asked – no, begged – him to fight, but he was just kinda done. There had been roughly a year from the diagnosis to his death. I wasn't really ready to have zero parents before 30, but it happened.

So there I was, at 34, with my older sister, my person, who I knew did her best to fight to stay. But the cancer was aggressive and once it metastasises to vital organs, it's pretty brutal. Gone.

After the first two death punches, I just flipped a switch and turned things on autopilot.

I walked back out, did my presentation, and then let the team know that I had to leave. Autopilot.

Smiling. Autopilot.

Breastfeeding. Autopilot.

Work. Autopilot.

Dinner. Autopilot.

Disconnection. Autopilot.

Flying to central Queensland. Autopilot.

Helping my 19-year-old niece speak about her mum. Autopilot.

Having déjà vu about my mum. Autopilot.

Speaking at her funeral. Autopilot.

Training for a half-marathon (yes, I managed to do this). Autopilot.

As is the case with putting things on autopilot, eventually you look up and wonder where the heck you are, or where the heck you went.

I found myself on the top floor of a car park after dropping little miss Abby at daycare. I had driven to the top floor of the car park deliberately because people only really sought out the top floor of the car park if the rest of the car park was full. After all, it was exposed to the elements. Birds could come and crap on your car and add another to-do to your already long list of to-dos. No one really parked at the top. Which is why it seemed like the perfect place to go.

I had even stopped at a little corner store in South Melbourne and bought a packet of cigarettes, despite not even smoking. Stupid idea, really.

As my autopilot came to a halt, I sat in the car wondering how the fuck did I end up in this shit pile of just hating my life, despite the fact I had an awesome baby? I mean, I'd run a motherfucking half-marathon – with a pram.

Yet I was deeply and utterly unhappy. The disconnection. The switching off. The hamster wheel I had subscribed to with the outward projection of 'Belle is doing great' whereas Belle was not doing so great. Belle – the real Belle – was dying while she was living. But not living. Just existing.

I packed up the grief while I tried to be a mum, and a worker, and a partner, and didn't really allow myself to grieve for my older sister until 2018. But back then, I was not in that space.

The weird, sad thing is that when the universe death punches you a couple of times, you start to realise that maybe things are not all right with the world, and that maybe, just maybe, you have to fight for yourself.

That day in the car park was a tipping point.

What kind of mother was I going to be, if I wasn't going to be brave? Not brave in terms of fighting lions and tigers and sharks – although I'd totally go all mumma bear if anything tried to harm my young, but brave in terms of fighting for the happy. Fighting for me.

As I sat there and ugly cried in my blue Subaru, I lit a Peter Stuyvesant and stared at the smoke snaking up into the air, watching it burn down to a stub. I knew deep down that something had to change.

I was in no position to quit my job – the big-arse mortgage made sure of that.

Becoming a yoga teacher was not going to pay the big-arse mortgage either. Plus, I would need a couple years of consistent practise, and that was not on the table with two working parents.

I guess recognising that something has to change is a gift. I'm lucky that I caught my downward spiral when I did. When the universe death punches you a couple times, you become – if you are lucky – a little more aware of the signs to watch for in others, and in yourself.

Staring at a burning cigarette as I sat in my blue Subaru on a rooftop car park was one of those 'you better change something or you are going to be thinking about worse things than smoking a stupid cigarette' moments.

I don't know if I would call it a moment of clarity. I would call it a moment of crystallisation, though.

Through life, I had made a couple of promises.

Don't turn out like Mum.

Don't turn out like Dad.

Don't miss out on things like Witchy did.

The biggest, most important one, though: Do Not Quit On Life. Fight. No matter how hard getting back up is, get back up. Chumbawamba 'Tubthumping' style. Tubthump it all the way to old age. I mean, I have an old lady goals Pinterest board. Long, flowing grey hair. Leather pants. Muscles, not frailty. No pancake butt. Maybe get arrested for streaking. No early check-outs.

I looked in the mirror and did not recognise who I was looking at. I didn't recognise the personality – it had morphed into some corporate grey pantsuit who didn't give a shit about themselves. I had totally frumped out and checked out of being happy.

I knew I needed to fight for a connection back to me more than anything.

Things needed to change on the work front.

Throwing away the cigarettes, I reached out to Jaq and another coach. I started looking at the escape plan a little more. Even though it would take a couple years for it to be born, I figured workingmumcoach.com could be something. I could design my life my way.

A move got planned. We left my beloved Melbourne – land of affordable coffee, awesome friends and beautiful shoes – and moved. I left my corporate safety net. That kind of 'back yourself' jump feels like you just jumped out of a plane and are hoping to God that your parachute opens, so you don't have a financial kamikaze. Cue the birth of my business and Mumpreneur – the program Jo was talking about.

I'm thankful for friends like Jo – she's like a sister to me.

The day is about to get away, though – it's either ring her back now while it's still early in the morning and before the breakfast chaos kicks off with the kids, or wait until later in the day. I choose before the chaos.

Jo answers FaceTime. She's driving in the car with her phone stuck in a phone holder on the dash.

"I've got like 15 minutes until I hit a dead patch, so go... where were we? Getting started."

"Oh, yeah. Well, I'd figured that any mum trying to do business and be a mum was probably working from home and isolated, so the programs would be a good solution."

"Well that's true. Hey, are you still in touch with that woman – you know, the horse masseuse?"

"Yeah – she moved to Europe. I'm in touch with her on LinkedIn. You were a fan, hey."

"Yeah not so much. Hahaha, OMG. But there were lots of really cool people."

"True – the friendships and community that have bubbled up and out of that little program for me and for others just fills me with purpose and joy. I mean, you are stuck with me like a belly button gets stuck with lint!"

"Belle, gross. You need to wash that shit out. Belly buttons can stink. So where are things at?"

"Well, every year, I still worry that there will be no participants. That I'll be done. And I'll end up dressed as one of those giant koalas with a red charity bucket in Fremantle collecting money for The Wilderness Society."

"Hey, I've done that before. You don't want to do that. It does smell like a belly button in those things. Especially in summer." She snort laughs.

"I guess I'm concerned mostly because I have just dropped the $10K on the air con in the last couple of months. Plus, I know there is a tax bill to come and I'm going to the States, and Thailand and Singapore this year. And there is no other financial net. I *am* the net. But hey, I've asked for money before. I know how to hustle. I can channel my inner poker face, and hustle and do it again."

"Hey, I'm almost home. About to hit a dead patch. I'll ring you back in 10 or 40."

And just like that she is gone. I use our chat break to remember what I have done, been through and overcome before.

When I found myself in single parentdom, my very, very old blue Subaru died on the side of the road on a 40-degree day in spectacular fashion. A new car was no longer simply on the cards – it was being smoke-signalled at me from the hissing engine, with two kids in car seats wondering what was going on.

I'd just been approved with my mortgage, so I didn't really want any more debt. My choice, though, was push bike and public transport with little kids, or a new car and make more money. I chose option two. We always have a choice.

I had a corporate planning day to negotiate the following week and had been loaned a car to get there. It was the first of many big asks.

They had wanted me to facilitate a strengths team-building day for them. I kind of had a sense as to what was charged for a full day of facilitation. I knew it depended on how I articulated my value. There was really only one way to figure it out, though. I needed a number.

With everything else feeling like it had turned to shit in my life, I wasn't sure if I could make it happen or not. But I think it kind of helped that, in my mind, I had to believe. I had to push the envelope. I had looked at all the things I had been through – I was resilient. I was resourceful. And I had a good track record in negotiating during my cubical career days.

I knew if I was too low with my price, the yes would be an easy yes. If I was too high, I would lose out.

I sat with the blue suits, the balding heads and the young female assistant who diligently took notes. I sat in my pink shirt, black pants and leopard print, so-not-corporate flats – I didn't want to get my full business pants personality back out on display.

Listening is always key. Listen in for their problem. Ask what they would like the outcome to be.

So there I sat, waiting to offer my solution to their situation. Ready to feel the fear about how much I valued myself, and whether I could walk the walk with money as the energy exchange.

"Great, this is what I can do for you. For me to do this, it will be $3800."

Poker face on the outside. *Holy shitballs, did I just ask for over $3000?* on the inside.

Their reaction was great. It wasn't a straight yes. It was a "Oooh, well, that might be outside our budget."

Also fine with me. So what did I do? I ladyballsed up and negotiated.

"Okay, well for me to fit within your budget, we can remove this component here, or I'm open to suggestions on what else you would like to do."

The blue suits suggest, "What if we reduce the time – can we reduce the fee? Then we can let you go at 2 pm."

Secretly, inside, I am thinking, *This actually works better for me logistically, as I can make school pick up – sweet.*

Then, I go for the upsell.

"That is a great idea, blue suits. For you to get value out of our time, though, I'd highly recommend in future that we put the other session in as, in my experience workshopping, participants tend to show up, listen, go back and forget. If we set it so that they have some actions in between sessions, then that will help you get a good return out of your time, energy and investment."

"Okay, we will have fries with that."

"Excellent, thank you, blue suits. I'll see you soon."

As I left, I was thinking, *Holy shit! I can't believe they said yes! If I can do this once, I can do it again.*

So, note to self – remember that you have been bold at asking for money, believing in yourself, and you can do this again.

Jo's face pops up on my screen again. "Okay, right, back in range. Tell me, what do you need, Mumpreneur-wise?"

"Well, I will run at least one program. I've got enough for one, but more would be good. At least two. And what are you doing now?"

"I'm cooking mussels. There are heaps of them down on the shore. I like taking Claire down to collect them, and I've debearded them so now they are cooking on the fire. Saves electricity. So, tell me. What can I do? I've still got a big following on Insta over there. Want me to do a post?"

I watch her wander back to the black pot. The billy? The stoneware thing on the fire.

"Jo? What is that pot on the fire?"

Jo comes up to her phone. Gives me the look like I'm an idiot.

"It's a pot, idiot."

"I know it's a pot, dickhead. What type of pot?"

"Oh, I don't know the brand if that's what you mean. It's cast iron. Op-shop find. Anyway, want me to post something? When are you going to come see me and we can do a workshop here?"

"That would be great, I'd appreciate that. I'll try to figure it out. Not this year. Maybe next year. Hey, how's everything going? Are you okay?"

"Yeah, good. There are a few things I'm processing in my head right now, but I'll tell you about that later. I can't talk about that right now. So what's happening with this chap, what's his name? Hot Hands? Have you seen him again?"

"Huh. Yeah. OMG, talk about awkward. Know how I told you that Lauren and I went pole dancing, and we have, like, a 'be brave and do stuff' list?"

"Yeah, have you started learning to surf yet?"

"Oh, my God – I can't wait! Starts this week. Actually, I'd better run. I can hear the kids up and about. Chat later."

"Okay cool. Bye! Hey – I want to hear!"

Approaching a surfer is intimidating. I think it goes back to high school, when somehow you started classifying yourself and the 'others'. Sometimes you accidentally feed yourself stories from the past that don't help your future. Arty type – not me. Sporty type – not me. Back then, none of us really knew what was going on in our home lives. We would only see what was in front of us. So, I guess I'm working to break down any other barrier stories my brain has created about stereotypes of others and my own self-worth. I need to get over myself.

Having a little boy, I really have no bearing on 'boy life'. I'm also super-conscious of all the 'girl power' messages in our household – what is that doing to him that he is not saying? I want both my kids to know they can do anything, so it's best I go find out how. I don't really know a lot about surf culture or skate culture, so I'm up for trying both. For now, surfing, because water is way softer than concrete.

I'm down at the surf club, heading out for a quick swim, and I spot Surf Dundee's van. He's about to pack up and take his boards back.

"Hey, I'm Belle. Have you got five minutes before you go?"

"Hey! Nice ta meet ya. Sure, I can spare a sec, but then I've gotta run as I've got someplace to be."

"Won't take long. Can you maybe teach me and my friend Lauren how to surf?"

"When are ya thinking you want ta learn?"

"Maybe Thursday mornings? How much is it?"

"Depends on how many of ya's there are. If it's a group, I can probably do a deal."

His eyes squint in the sun. He has that cheeky 'I'm going to tell it like it is' grin.

"At this stage, only two of us."

"Okay, well, it'll be $20 each, and we'll see how we go. Have you surfed before?"

"Nope – it's been on the list to learn most of my life, so I want to learn."

"Can you be down at the surf club at 9 on a Thursday?"

"Can we make it 9:30? Lauren, my friend, is coming from Mandurah."

Thursday rolls around, and Lauren and I take ourselves down to the beach. It's overcast. It's choppy. For beginner surf conditions, it does not look ideal. We grab our softboards and a couple of wetsuits each and follow Surf Dundee down to the beach.

He's really quite a character. He explains how to read the water and look for rips, so that we can choose a safe space to learn. The advice is to not go past waist-high water to make it easier for getting on the board.

I feel a little Keanu Reeves in *Point Break* (but not as cool) as I start on the sand, learning hand placement, working out whether I'm natural or goofy foot and looking for my mark. Note to self: get contact lenses, as the tiny bit of dried-up sex wax on my blue board which is my mark is really hard to spot without glasses. Our hands dig little channels in the sand next to our boards, as Surf Dundee teaches what is really a little bit of a yoga-type move. Push up (baby cobra). Drag your front leg forward, pull the other leg to the side and in, and pop into a warrior pose. Oooh, yeah. Wave warrior.

A few shots of practising on the sand, and we are into the choppy waves. Whenever I put a wetsuit on (and I have not put one on since my pre-kid triathlon days) I feel like a superhero. An out-of-shape superhero at the moment, but still a superhero. A superhero about to take on Mother(fucker) Nature, who has actual superpowers that will take you down.

I was born without hand-eye coordination – at least that's what I was told by my physical education teacher in ninth grade, and again by my first boyfriend who was studying to be a physical education teacher, and who lost his shit at me while trying to teach me to play squash. He's now a finance broker, probably a good thing. I do have decent balance. I can run in a straight line, and am a bit of a water baby, so I figured I'd get this surf thing.

Out Lauren and I go, with Surf Dundee following suit to explain how to get on a board.

"Right, you are going to glide onto the board, so watch your hand placement, push forward with the wave to catch it and then try to stand up. Make sure your nose hits your mark."

What mark? I can see it even less now that we are in the water.

Surf Dundee helps one of us at a time. Lauren first, then me. He also gives adult feedback that is pretty straightforward.

I go to get on my board. My body-slap on the board is audible. Like a dolphin has breached, except I don't have the grace of a dolphin.

Surf Dundee booms above the waves. "Whaddya call that? I said glide on the board! That's not gliding! That's flopping on it like a wet fish!"

Now, unfortunately for me, I get the giggles at the, um, 'constructive feedback', which just makes it even harder to see where my mark is.

Surf Dundee yells, "Get off the board and try again."

I oblige. I'm too far back on my board this time. I can't see the wax where my nose should be.

"Oi! Girly – you missed ya mark! Try again."

No one has called me girly in a long time. And I don't know that Lauren and I can work out whether our larrikin of a surf coach is in his forties or his sixties due to his beautiful leather sea-weathering from a life in the sun.

I try, and this time succeed in hitting the mark and not wet-fish flopping. Looking up, I see an approving thumbs-up. Getting up is a different story. I try and get to half a wave warrior, when Mother Nature – or more probably (okay, certainly) my lack of skill – takes me down. Dundee of the Sea has also taught us that hands go up first in case the board comes back and smacks you. I forget this part, and the board comes back along the leg rope and gets me just beneath the eye.

I'm grateful it's a softboard. Softboards aren't so soft when they surf punch you in the face, though. Lesson learned. Hands go up next time.

The first round of surfing sees Lauren get to her feet, but I fail. We agree to go again the following week. I'm fine with failing for fun if it's something I'm interested in doing.

Back to the beach for week two.

Surf Dundee comes out to help us wrestle our softboards and start catching waves. He returns to the sand to watch what we are doing, yelling sporadically, "You missed ya mark," "Nup," "What do you call that?" followed by "You (pointing at me) – get out of the water and come and practise on the sand."

Yep – you can get benched for shitty surf skills.

I practise again on the sand, until Surf Dundee is okay with me getting back out there.

Back out I go, attempting and failing at catching a wave. I completely miss it. And from a distance, I hear the following loud and clear:

"THAT WAS SHIT, GIRLY!"

I can't do anything but laugh. I'm determined not to give up.

I watch Lauren (who has brought her rock god husband along) and she gets up and rides the wave in, with yells of "Woohoo! I did it!" This is quickly followed by, "Okay, I'm done."

Lauren returns to the beach with her rock god husband while I work at catching the next one.

Eventually, with enough perseverance and enough dunks from my friend the green lady, I catch one, get my wave warrior pose on and stay standing for two whole seconds!

I did it!

I don't care if it's only two seconds. I did it. I go back out again and again and again until Surf Dundee calls time and says that I will be tired.

He talks about energy management and points to the 'real' surfers sitting out the back on their boards, telling me that as I've been going back and forth, I'll be tired and sore the next day.

I ask him about getting a surfboard, and what does he recommend. Turns out Dundee is a fan of getting on Gumtree and looking for a big Mal.

"Just keep getting out here, girly – as much as you can before winter kicks in. Then the waves are just going to be shit and rough and choppy and that's no fun. But keep trying. There were no such things as surf coaches when I learned. We just got a board and went and figured it out."

I commit to keep up my ocean-going habits, especially on a Thursday before I have to do the ballet-mum Uber-driver run with my daughter.

The next day is training with Becs. I figure I'll be fine after the surf. My body says otherwise. My right hamstring (my back surfing leg) is super-tight. I start to do some circuits, but have to pull out of squats and lunges as I feel like my hamstring is about to ping. Becs races over. "I think you should go for acupuncture before you make it worse."

She has no idea that I have a crush on her friend. I really don't want to make another appointment yet. I'm not ready for the heart type of awkward bravery.

Remembering my total dork-out last time I saw Baker, I go through my network to find who else I can go see for help. This is a definite bonus of the work I do, helping mums get their businesses going. I know loads of peeps. Photographers, massage therapists, accountants, bloggers, bakers, candlestick makers. For real. The downside of this is, I teach them to build businesses around the life they want. This means, unfortunately for me, that my calls go like this:

Calls a masseuse I know named Toni.

Toni's answering machine: "Thanks for your call. We are currently taking a break for two weeks over the summer, and will be back on deck later. Stay safe and enjoy the sunshine."

Damn it. *Calls a Bowen therapist I know named Jasmine.*

Jasmine's message service: "Hey! We are currently on holidays. If your body is not as strong as you need it right now, we recommend you call City Chiropractors on blah blah blah who have limited sessions available."

Shit, shit, shit. Stupid hamstrings and back.

I call two more women I know from my programs. Turns out, they all listened to me on the 'planning the business around enjoying life' front. Which is great, but sucks to be me right now with this hamstring and back issue. I do not want the sciatica to be an ongoing thing. I call the chiropractor near my house. I call the physio. All on a break. Probably with the dentist in the Bahamas.

Shit. I know he's good at what he does. Maybe he will be unavailable.

Out comes the phone, and off goes the text message to Baker. He is available.

The appointment gets booked for Monday while my daughter is at ballet. Talk about being an Uber driver for my kids. My kids and my awkwardness. Yay.

~~~~~

I'm honestly surprised I manage to get dressed for my Monday appointment.

"What were you doing to put yourself in this kind of pain?"

"Started to learn to surf with Lauren. And then did a session with Becs."

"Okay. Let's get you on the table and see if we can take some of this pain away. Are you going to be okay getting yourself there?"

"I guess so."

"Well, yell out if you need help. I'll be just outside."

God, I hope so. I don't really want to be assisted by Mr Hotness in undressing myself and getting onto the massage table.

He exits the studio and leaves me to gingerly remove everything but briefs and bra and lie facedown with a large, fluffy grey towel over my back. It takes me nearly eight minutes to do this, with a couple of 'are you going okay's' coming from Baker.

The worst part about any acupuncture chats is being facedown. I can't read any body language. But then, I guess, maybe it's better than being face-up where I'll dork out and have to make eye contact and worry about whether my head looks like a potato because my face will fall backwards or I'll say stupid things like, "So, do you like stuff? I like stuff." Either way, I am feeling very, very vulnerable being in excruciating pain on a massage table with this lovely hot person who I have tried to avoid seeing, and who is about to stick needles in my back. And my brain, as it turns out.

"So, how is that list going?"

"Great, thanks. I am definitely going to go to Vegas for a work thing and go hike the Grand Canyon, so I really want to get my back and legs sorted. Have you been?"

"Yes, I have, it's pretty incredible. I think the word I would use to describe it is magnificent. Well, the beauty there is grand, so grand is probably a good word for it."

"I can't wait to go. I kinda want to hike all the way down to the bottom and hike out, but I'm not sure if I will have enough time to do it or not."

"Just get yourself super-fit so you can go."

"Working on it. We just happen to live in a very flat part of the world. I found it much easier to get out and hike when I lived in Melbourne, as you could drive an hour out of the city and end up in either the Dandenong Ranges or Mount Macedon. Anywhere, really."

"I'm just going to place a few needles in. Just be ready."

Good thing Bakes can't see my face right now, as it's kinda making a 'holy fuck this fucking hurts' expression, which looks like a scrunched up Medjool date that has been bleached white and given some teeth and eyes. Well, maybe not as wrinkly as a Medjool date, but I'd bet that it is not a pretty face shoved in the hole in the table.

My hands smack the resting space beneath my face as I let out an audible "aaah".

"Sorry, I know this is going to feel worse before it feels better."

He rests his hand on my shoulder, while I watch his feet walk past the hole in the table around to the right side and pop another needle in.

"So are you going by yourself to the Grand Canyon and Vegas?"

"Well, I started out going by myself for the mastermind, and was going to go and do the Grand Canyon myself, but then Sam, who is hosting the retreat, said she'd tag along. And Lauren is coming along, too."

"Sooo…. Is Lauren your life partner?"

Simultaneously, I analyse the question and answer. The comment sends my brain into overdrive. At this very moment that I am facedown in a hole, I am super-grateful. Had I been face-up, I don't think I could have controlled any of my 'what the fuck' facial expressions. I mean, do I give off a gay vibe? Why is he asking about whether Lauren is my life partner?

"No! She's my friend. Why would you ask if she is my life partner?"

"Well… you never know. I'm just finding things out. What if Lauren likes you?"

"Well, she is married to a rockstar-type husband, so I doubt that I'm her type. I'm pretty sure we are both #teampeen."

"But you are going to Vegas… What's the sleeping arrangement?"

I'm sure my face is beetroot red right now. I'm glad it's in this hole. I'm glad he cannot see the amount of muscle movement happening in my face that is relaying my brain's thoughts of, *What the fuck is happening?*

"We are sharing a bed, but hey, you know, what happens in Vegas… hahaha."

"Is she going to the Grand Canyon with you, too?"

"Yep. But I'm not sure if Sam and Lauren know that when I say I'm hiking for the whole day, I mean the actual whole day. Like, from sunrise to sunset."

"What will you do if they ditch you?"

"I won't care, to be honest. I'll just keep going and figure out how to meet them back wherever. It's a bonus that they are coming."

"Well, sounds like you have it sorted. So… Are you dating anyone, then, if Lauren is not your life partner?"

"Um, nope. You?" *What the fuck?*

"I wouldn't even know where to start. Not the online dating thing, I think those people are weird."

"My friend in Melbourne, Jaq, has done the online thing, so I hear what it's like from her. But I mean, how are you supposed to go on dates anymore when there is work and kids and stuff involved? What would you do?"

"I don't know… Pass a friend a note to pass another friend."

"Sixth-grade style, I like it. Maybe you can meet them at the roundabout after school."

"Yeah, I guess so. You must get asked out, though?"

"Um, no, not really. I work with 98 percent women in the work I do, and then it's all kid stuff, so not really unless it's the arty types who still live with their mums. Actually, I haven't even told my kids that I'm getting back out there."

"Oh, right. That sounds scary. Well, I guess it's a bit of a minefield out there. What else is on that list again?"

"Ahhh, I'm going to try to overcome my fear of frogs."

"That's right! I remember you mentioning that last time!"

I'm grateful that the conversation has turned back to something that doesn't scare me as much as talking about whether I am gay or not, and whether I am dating or not. I'm still overthinking, wondering, *Why all the questions?* I've never been asked so many personal questions facedown on a massage table in my mum undies before. Especially by someone so hot.

He removes the needles from my back and my legs and lets me know to take my time getting up and that he will come back in when I am dressed.

I pull what I call my comfy fat dress back on. It's grey. It's batwinged from about the upper thigh so that it's a one-size-fits-all dress. It was easy to get into without too much pain. I'm wearing Adidas trainers. They're kinda my comfy dance-mum-hanging-out-at-a-café clothes. The kind of dress that skims your boobs, but hides your belly. Shows off your legs, but hides your bumps. After that conversation, I'm really wondering if I am dressing like a lesbian. I mean, I find being tall hard enough. What if I give off a vibe, and I don't even know it?

Bakes comes back in and looks me up and down. Like in the 'you just got pictured without your grey dress on' look up and down. I fidget. He makes a comment about liking the kicks, and then shows me a few stretches to do, including sitting on the edge of the table and dropping my head while I lift my left leg, then my right leg, curving my back out.

"You should take some anti-inflammatories too, just to stop the muscles spasming."

"I don't even take Panadol – can't I just leave it?"

"I get it, but this is not going to get better without taking something. It needs heat, anti-inflammatories and the stretches. See how you go, and you may need to come back in a few days."

While my sciatica still hurts, it feels better. Except I am leaving with a different type of problem. I am super, super-confused. Why ask all those questions about whether I am gay, or whether I am dating anyone, or whether I am on online dating apps?

I do know one thing. It's a definite signal that I am ready to get back out there instead of sitting in my chickenshit shell being afraid. I also know that I need to talk to my kids. After all, meeting a new person could feel extremely awkward for them, too.

With a mental note about talking to the kids, I get in the car to pick up Abby from ballet, and phone Lauren immediately.

"Have you got five?"

"Sure – what's up?"

"Do you think I come off as gay?"

"No, why?"

"Well, I just saw the acupuncture guy, and he asked if you and I were life partners."

"Oh, Baker?"

"Lol – yes, that's him. I didn't think I gave off a gay vibe, but maybe I do. Not really the vibe I am going for."

"No, you don't give off a gay vibe. Do you think you might be gay?"

"No, definitely not. Doesn't even cross my mind. I mean, I think women are beautiful, but I don't think about women in that way. I'm happy to try loads of things and go to loads of places. Just don't want to go down to Lady Taco Town. I'm definitely team peen."

"Oh, Belle. You have a way with words. Maybe we should build a pillow wall in Vegas… hahaha."

"Oh, you never know. If it gets really cold in the Grand Canyon, we might need to snuggle for body warmth, given we will be camping in a tent. Hahaha. What do you think?"

I love Lauren. In a non-gay way. She pauses. I love how she stops and thinks through what to say before she says it.

"I think he likes you, and he was trying to suss things out."

"Really? Nooo. No way. That is sooo not a possibility. He's way too hot to like someone like me. God, this is bugging me. Maybe I need to rethink my whole wardrobe for Vegas if this is what the response is. Shit."

"Well, what are you going to do about it?"

"I don't know! Nothing, probably, except overthink things. Maybe I'll call Jo."

"Okay, well, go chat to Jo. See you soon?"

"Yep – I'll see you for the frog thing soon, okay?"

~~~~~~

I ring Jo for her level 10 honesty.

"Do you think I dress like I'm gay?"

"No, I think you dress like you're fat when you're not, but I don't think you look like you bat for the other team. But those giant fucking wedge shoes that you have on in your photo – they are not my thing at all. Get rid of them. They are hideous."

I chuckle. I love Jo. Not everyone can handle her type of honesty. I don't take her comments with offence. I take her comments with love, so I can equally turn around with this:

"Hahaha, God I love you. We've talked about the shoes. I'm not taking shoe advice from someone who thinks gumboots are the height of footwear sophistication. A lot of people actually love those shoes."

The shoes in question are leather cream Jeffrey Campbell wedges that lace up at the front. I freaking love them. I also own Hunter gumboots. I can tell you which ones get worn more.

"Well, I'm glad you've found some friends with equally poor taste in shoes. But hey, let's get back to this chat. Why do you think people think you dress like you're gay?"

I relay everything that has transpired, and my state of confusion.

"What state are your boobs in at the moment?" she randomly asks.

"What? What has that got to do with anything?"

"Well, I know you, and if your boobs are looking awesome, you are generally carrying a little more weight. So – what state are you in?"

"Oh, I'm on the heavy side right now. The boobs do look awesome."

"Maybe he's trying to suss things out. I think you should re-book and just ask and find out."

"I can't do that! I would die."

"Come on, isn't this your year of being fucking brave or something? You are going to have to be vulnerable, otherwise you are going to stay in this weird limbo space where you have no idea whether the comments were innocent or whatever. Send a text!"

I sit on this advice for a while and think about what I'm going to do. I mean, I'm certainly #teampeen, yet I don't want to be giving off the 'I like vaginas other than my own' vibe. It would be good to get a guy's view, though, as maybe I'm dressing completely the wrong way. I also want to sort this out before I go off to the States, or consider venturing into any dating space, online or otherwise. If there is one thing I've learnt from Bakes switching that little light back on, is that the light is back on and I need to start being brave and move on – one way or another.

Staring at my phone, I try to work out what to say, and I draft a message: *Hey, the comment about Lauren being my life partner really bugged me the other day, so I need your advice, and I'm really embarrassed to ask. Anyway... If how I'm dressing is giving off a gay vibe, then yay because it means I'll go shopping and change that, and if how I'm dressing is okay, then yay because I'll probably still go shopping, so whatever your comment is, it's a win-win, but I need a man's opinion as Lauren being my life partner is not the vibe I am going for (winky smiley face emoji).*

I stare at my phone and think about hitting send. Then I actually hit send and freak out. Then I ring Jo back again. My trusty cuts-to-the-chase-with-a-truthbomb bestie.

"I sent a text message."

"What did you say?"

I start to relay the whole thing, and then as I'm chatting, through comes a text response.

"Hang on, I've got a text back."

Bakes: *I'm sorry if I made you feel weird – thanks for letting me know, I'd never mean to hurt your feelings. You dress fine the way you are. Don't change anything.*

"Great!" says Jo after I read it to her. "So he doesn't think you're gay. He might be interested in you. You should go book back in for... what is it he does again? Acupressure or chiropractor or something?"

"Acupuncture."

"Whatever. Maybe I should have made his code name Pin Fingers."

"What? Pin Fingers?"

"Yeah, it narrows the whole alternate therapy thing down for me. You'd wanna hope he's not a pin dick, though – you never know. Hahaha."

"Jo! Can we stick to Hot Hands."

"Spoil sport! You should book back in and get over the awkwardness that you created, otherwise it's going to be pretty fucking weird next time. Make sure you wear nice knickers."

"Nope, not doing that. I'm daggying on down, as I don't want to even give off any kind of curiosity or anything. I'm too chickenshit. I'm not ready for that yet."

"I thought you are supposed to be brave this year?"

"I know. Maybe I'll go hold a frog. Let me tackle some of the other things to be brave with first. Plus, someone like him would never be interested in someone like me. He's like part of the leading-man movie cast – I'm part of, well, not that."

"Oh, shit, the kids have just... wait, why is the chicken inside the house? Belle, I've gotta go. Send a text. Invite him for a surf. It's not like it's a marriage proposal. Remember! Bravery!"

She hangs up. That is the beauty of our friendship. If someone has to go mid-sentence, we just hang up. We try not to, but sometimes it happens. Life happens. Bad phone reception happens. Work happens. Chickens inside your house happens. There is enough understanding, trust, respect and humour that things are easy, even when we have gone through periods of having to sort shit out mentally. If one of us asks for space in terms of no contact for 30 days, then we oblige. If one of us asks for support for 30 days because we have hit an emotional ditch, then we check in a lot more. Not to do anything but to process things on the phone.

Another text comes through:

Bakes: *So, how is the pain going?*

Me: *Still sore, but better.*

Bakes: *Well, you should come back in if it's still sore in a couple of days.*

Me: *Thanks I will do.*

But I don't. I don't invite him for a surf. I don't go back in a few days. I dodge the whole thing. I put my embarrassment in a box and pack it away, telling myself that it's better left alone before I make more of a dick of myself. Plus, I need to speak to the kids.

I know I'm ready to get back out there, as scary as it seems. The conversation with the kids about the possibility of me dating again needs to happen. For some reason, the planned tricky conversations with the kids feel way more awkward and hard to me compared to the random ones where they just drop bombs on you in the car and you have to explain erections or testicles or sex.

I guess this marks the start of them experiencing awkwardness. Cue life lessons from your mother. I know they will thank me in the future, when they need to be brave.

It is nothing short of a weird conversation to navigate. I weigh up the pros and cons of telling the kids I am thinking about dating, or not telling them and going all secret squirrel on their butts to one day spring a 'hey, meet your potential bonus dad' situation on them. There seems to be no right or wrong answer.

One morning on a Saturday, the kids start a pillow fight on my freshly made bed. They crawl underneath my doona, making a tunnel. They are having fun, and I'm outnumbered. I'm trying to work up the courage to do the whole online dating app thing with the support of Jaq. I look at their little faces, and have my final internal debate on whether I tell them, or just leave it.

"Ahem! Sooo. I want to chat with you guys about Mum maybe making some new friends."

My son has high energy. He bounces up and down, doing a front flip toward me.

"What do you mean?" he says.

"Well, I mean that I might go out on dates this year."

My daughter stops bouncing, plops on the bed and grabs a pillow. "Mum! Why are you telling me this? That's gross! Lalalalalalala! I don't want to hear you!"

"I want to see you kiss people!" Bear says. "Yay! Go on dates! Go on dates! Go on dates!"

Clearly, there is team mumgoesonadate and team mumgetseatenbycats.

"Well, you won't meet anyone I date unless they are a nice person, so don't get too excited."

"Eeew," says Abby. "Gross. Why do you have to tell me this? It's disguuuusting! I don't want to know. But is it because you are lonely? You shouldn't be lonely, you have us and your friends."

"Well, I'm trying to be honest, because I figure that, say, I do date someone, and then eventually you meet them, you would be like, 'Oh, why didn't you say anything?'"

This is stressful. My face fills with stress at the thought of traumatising my kids before I have even met someone for a coffee. I feel like this is a no-win situation with my daughter.

"Can't you, like, talk to your mum friends about this? This is horrible. I don't want to think about it! When are you seeing Lauren? What about Jo? They can help you."

"Abs, I don't know – it's not like I've got a book on how to have a conversation with your kids about dating. I haven't had to do this before. And I am talking to my mum friends, but I figured it would be best to tell you guys."

"Go on dates! Go on dates! Go on dates!" Bear jumps up and down on the bed, cheering me on. I think he would just like the boys and girls in the house evened out.

"Bear, stop it! I don't want a new dad."

"Baby girl, you will never get a new dad. Dad will always be your dad. One day, though, you and your brother will grow up and go to live amazing, happy lives, and I'm going to need someone to do your chores, like unpack the dishwasher."

I tickle her and poke her in the ribs. She gets my joke.

"Muuum! Stooop!"

"Well, I'm just keeping you in the loop, so I won't tell you anything else now, but now you know. I love you."

"Love you too. Can we talk about something else now?"

"Sure. Hey, guess what. I'm going to try and overcome my fear this weekend!"

Bear squeals. "Froggies! Yay! Can we come?"

"No, baby boy. You are at Dad's house this weekend. He will have loads of fun stuff for you, I'm sure."

I park the online dating profile and go for something less scary on the list. Well, for now, anyway. I choose the frog.

4

APRIL

*P*roject bravery keeps going. My surfing keeps going. Not Lauren – Lauren ditches surfing – but the whole goal is to try new things and be brave, not to keep doing things that we decide we don't like anymore.

Lauren chats to a friend of hers and organises for me to face my fear.

During a Facebook Live.

Facebook Lives are something on Lauren's list to be brave with. The very first one we did after pole dancing, I was cracking jokes with her, watching her hands shake as we live streamed from my office. Jokes are my fallback. Laugh at me, and you aren't worrying about anything else. Laugh with me, and we'll be friends for life. I'm comfortable being the goofball. It's my best defence mechanism.

The firsts of anything, or the unfamiliars of anything, always feel weird. Or the return to something when it has been absent. You don't know what's changed, whether it will feel what home should feel like, or whether it will feel completely foreign and you'll wonder if you are an alien on another planet.

Because of my kids being with their dad this particular Friday night, we have opted to Facebook Live from Lauren's house, with a few friends to help us up our game. Including Toni – or ToTo, as I like to call her – who totally geeks out over tech and cameras and is one of the funniest people I know. She's got this new fancy camera called a something-something that follows you as you film. She's also a friend I collected through the Mumpreneur programs.

Walking into Lauren's house, I hear a familiar voice in the kitchen. Turns out Lauren's friend, Hector, who runs Beasties as Buddies, is someone I know. Hector is also the keeper of frogs. I know him from our boys going to daycare together a few years earlier. He breeds bearded dragons and other reptiles that my kids saw at his son's birthday party. Today, he's dressed a bit like Steve Irwin – you know, traditional 'I love nature' khaki, tall, about six foot three. And a face that is like… well, I guess if Bear Grylls and Steve Irwin loved it up, then ate the sad Care Bear – you know, the one with the raincloud – for survival purposes, they'd make Hector. I remembered him being way more like the sunshine Care Bear, though.

"So," I ask Hector, "is Lauren going first? Like with a spider or something?"

"Oh, you mean Harriet the huntsman? No, Harriet isn't here tonight."

He looks down at his beer, looking very sad. I recognise that sad. And it's not 'the absence of Harriet the huntsman' sad. It's 'my dream just died' sad. I park that thought as we all talk about how this is going to roll.

"Oh, shame. Harriet and I could have waxed our legs together."

Toni laughs. Lauren smiles and looks at Hector, then at me. She mouths the words, "He's not so great today."

"Okay. How are we going to do this?"

"Well, I hear this is all for you to overcome your fear of frogs," Hector says.

I feel my heartbeat already increase as my body tenses up. Fuck. That. Phobia.

"Are you trying to induce a flashback?"

"I'm a professional, Belle. I help people overcome their fears of bearded dragons and snakes and spiders all the time. It's a thing."

I stare at the boxes parked near the dining table, to the right of the kitchen bench.

"Are you packing a bearded dragon? Let's get one of those out. What about with frogs – have you helped people with fears of frogs? I think I'm gonna vomit."

"Look, to be honest, Belle, no bullshittin' you... frogs are not that common a fear. But I promise, you'll get through it."

Give me a snake or a spider any day. But frogs? I am so scared of those. It seems like a good place to start, and really, in the list of my things to do to be brave, I'd put this as easier on the vulnerability list then actually revealing any hint of, 'Hey, I might like you, Baker, but I'm not sure if you like me back.'

Now, I know people have fears over all sorts of things. Some of the more common ones are public speaking – which I am fine with – spiders, heights, getting naked after babies with a changed body (hellooo other hard thing for me to do), and leaving a situation because staying is a known, as unhappy as you may be. Then there are weirder fears. Like frogs.

I'm really, really conscious that I don't want to pass on any of my 'stuff' to my kids. I don't want them to grow up with my fear of frogs. For the most part, I think frogs are lovely. Except their unpredictability with their jumping.

I developed this fear thanks to my dear old dad. Parenting in the early '80s and beyond was just a little more... relaxed? Without rules? Maybe there were hangovers from the free-love '70s that saw parents care, but not really think about whether their actions would psychologically damage their kids.

***

Before my parents had their bitter divorce, we lived across from a lake. Actually, my dad stayed in the house, sometimes letting his bitterness towards my mum – with good reason – be fuelled on a Saturday at about 11 am by scotch on the rocks. Sometimes his humour was fuelled by his jester soul, where movies and radio shows would be made of mad dentists using electric can openers. I think he kept the house until he died as a show of stability. It really was the only permanent place in my life, even though I only lived there every second weekend.

I was also scared of the lake across the road from our house. Normally, when you picture a lake house, you imagine vast expanses of water, bird life and tranquillity. In my mind, though, the lake was a place full of dares and dangers. And fucking frogs. Scary-arse frogs.

I'm sure I remember my dad telling me that the lake was surrounded by quicksand. Couple that with an old black-and-white movie of *Tarzan* where someone was going to die, and I was convinced from about five years old that my life would be short-lived – probably due to the quicksand. He also told me that no one had ever been able to measure the bottom of the lake, which, as writing, I just googled and it's like 15 metres deep – so not a bottomless lake. Plus, apparently there were whirlpools in the middle that would suck you down and drown you, and three kids had died in there.

Tranquil my fucking arse. I was living across the road from an early grave. Yet those daredevil, risk-taking roots were there from an early age. I'd run across the road barefoot and navigate my way through the rushes and the rocks to where the sand would start to squish and squelch. I'd put my foot down into the 'quicksand' and watch as my left foot started to disappear, only to pull it out really quickly and go running, screaming, back to the house, with my tales of surviving the deadly quicksand, told only to the stuffed animals in my room, as had my dad found out, I'd be in the shit.

I don't know how any experts would describe his parenting style, except for potentially 'typical of the era'. Kids were as much for the amusement of parental jokes as possible. Magical worlds were created with hidden dangers, since there was no technology except maybe a colour TV if you were really lucky – one where you had to turn the knob to change the channel, and the 'Program does not commence until 7 am' multi-coloured thing would sit there while you awaited the arrival of *The Wombles*, or anything else.

I actually loved that magical world, and that was something that, despite my dad's flaws, I loved and cherished most about him. With the exception of the fucking frogs.

I really would have appreciated the frogs having frog parents that told them, "Don't go over to the house across from the lake. It contains lawnmowers that will chop you into a million pieces. There's a dog in the yard, and something called a dad that will include you in a sick game of chasey with his eldest kid."

I guess the frog sprogs had the same curious nature as me – look at that, something in common with my archnemesis. They inevitably ended up in the swimming pool out the back. Lord knows why they would want to be there. It was a thousand times smaller than the lake. Maybe they were into gated communities, or early adopters of minimalism or downsizing. Maybe they heard that chlorine had anti-ageing properties. Maybe they had big-arse daddy frogs who were into pranking them as their parental rite of passage.

I don't know how many times the following event happened, but eventually one stand-out frog-chasing moment ended up seared into my brain, cementing the fear and the phobia in some weird, tormented union.

I had spotted a frog. I'm sure it was 25 metres long and 10 metres wide. Okay, maybe not. I do think it was bigger than my head. I'd called out to dad that there was a frog in the pool. I wouldn't dare set foot in the pool with a frog in there. I was sure they were beelining for me with their big, bulgy eyes and would bite me if they got close enough. If I wasn't going to die a slow, torturous death by quicksand at the lake, then I was more than likely going to die from a poisonous frog bite. They weren't even poisonous.

Dad came out and fished the offending frog out of the pool using the mesh pool scoop we used to collect fallen hibiscus leaves out of the water. I was sure he was going to fling it from the pool scoop, over the house and back to the lake where it belonged.

Nope. No, no, no. Before I could even hit the frog-free water, he reached down, picked up the frog and held one of its front legs in each hand.

"BLURGHROROROROGHWGOEOSRORBLUR," Dad yelled, chasing me with the ginormous green-and-gold-speckled frog – who, I'm sure at the same time wished he'd listened to his frog parents' stories of the dangers of the house across the road and playing child chasey with the dark-haired, big-bellied man.

I don't think I remember ever screaming that loud, or moving that fast, in my entire life. I think I made myself airborne as I scooted into the house, into the lockable toilet in the laundry, which I locked, crying for two hours – maybe two weeks – while I heard Dad laugh as he took the frog back across the road to the lake.

I know I got out of the toilet, as I'm now a grown-arse woman, but I still to this day have no recollection of leaving the toilet to return to what should have been a safe space.

I have been scared of frogs for all my life, driving off the road when I see teeny, tiny ones out in the rain on the road in case they somehow magically make their way through the air vents.

Size does not matter when it comes to frogs. Big, small, fat, green, yellow, brown tadpole at the growing legs stage… my fear has no discrimination when it comes to frogs. The only acceptable ones are made of chocolate. Named Freddo. Or a peppermint Haigh's one.

Two little girls I looked after at my dad's house tested this theory out when I was a teenager. They found one no bigger than a thumbnail out the back. I don't even remember the names of these two evil little tyrants. Okay, they weren't evil, they were rather cute and thought this big, supposedly cool teenage girl who they looked up to would not be scared of frogs.

They carried him carefully up to the back porch only to see me fly through the laundry, once again to the safety of the toilet, where I locked the door.

But the two tiny bitches had other ideas. You see, there was a gap under the toilet door. A gap big enough to fit a tiny brown frog the size of a thumbnail.

Their giggles hinted that my panic room was about to be compromised. I'd been sitting perched on the toilet with the lid down. Door locked. Before I knew it, bouncing in came a tiny frog, sending me into hysterics. Not the laughing kind or the crying kind – the screaming kind. God, even now my heart rate goes up. My screams, however, did send the two little girls into hysterics – the laughing kind – at the sight of this gangly teenager jumping out of the toilet, over the tiny frog, through the kitchen, out the front door and into my car, keys in hand, where I locked the doors. I sat there as the two ice-cream-and-chocolate-sprinkle complexioned, sweet-faced evil geniuses stood smirking with their tiny amphibian power in their hands.

I didn't even crack my window to say goodbye. I yelled through the glass, "Tell my dad I had to go."

As I reversed out the driveway, I saw them standing there laughing their little heads off.

Scared of frogs. That is me.

I've tried to overcome this fear before. Heck, there is even an unpublished children's book about me trying to overcome this fear.

Due to my adventurous spirit and love of exploring, I took the day off after I turned 21 and headed to North Queensland to spend time with

Witchy before hitting the US and the UK, and other parts of Europe – wherever my backpacking, free-loving spirit wanted to go. What I wasn't thinking about with my move to the tropics was the presence of frogs. And toads. Weirdly, though, I am not as scared of toads. They don't stick. They don't jump great heights, and if I am being honest, I had no issue at all lining up those cane toads with my beat-up old blue Celica that I bought for $500 in Cairns and hearing them pop under my car tyres. Gross, I know. I'm just being honest – I'm not perfect. They are a pest and have destroyed more fauna in Australia than anything else. Cane toads have no natural predator in Australia, except for humans who actively work to take them out with their blue Celica tyres. I know it sounds mean. I know some well-intentioned but not-fully-thinking-it-through doobs brought them to Australia, and really, it's not the cane toad's fault that they ended up here. The toads ended up on a toad vacay fuelled by an all-you-can-eat invite to chow down on the native Australian cane beetle that was destroying sugar cane crops. The toads did not succeed here, but they also topped off their migration with basically a toad orgy that produces between eight and 35 thousand (yes, thousand – ew, gross) toady-poles a pop.

With all the excitement about spending time with my older sister and building a relationship with her, I didn't even think about the fact that I was packing my fear and taking it to Frogageddon. What was I thinking? Truth be told, I was thinking I'd be gone for a year, spend most of it overseas and then go back west.

I was wrong. I loved North Queensland. Even the frogs. I white-water rafted, hiked through rainforests, learned to waterski on freshwater rivers containing crocs (the '80s-style parenting was not lost on my older sister and her then-husband), swam in isolated waterholes, slept under stars, jumped off cliffs into gorges, dated cowboys, mustered cattle, dated Canadian backpackers, left a kneecap on a blackwood tree four hours from ranch in the middle of nowhere bumfuck Idaho and discovered that if you haven't severed an artery, no one is coming for your football-sized knee. And I learned to sail. Life was great.

Sailing is a great skill to learn. As much as the sport requires money, boats require a crew – generally without the money. It's social, and you become known as a 'grotty yachty'. You need to be able to communicate, work as a team, take directions, read the wind and drink like, well, a sailor.

The friendships through sailing were great – even though I'm no longer connected as I once was to my crew.

The ribbing that occurred with the crew I belonged to over my fear of frogs actually had me try to face up to it, as opposed to calling upon someone to come and perform a frog extraction for me.

Even though my doors were closed in the little Queenslander cottage I lived in, somehow, this tiny frog – no bigger than the one the two little girls had shoved under the toilet door all those years ago – found its way into my house. And onto the toilet seat.

It sat there as I raced home from a twilight sail on a Wednesday night, busting for the toilet. I would have been 25, I guess. And wearing a mini-skirt. God knows why I was wearing a mini-skirt and not shorts that day, but it was the tropics. It was hot, and I was going to pee my pants if I didn't get to my toilet on time.

In I raced to see this little green dude sitting on the white rim of the toilet. No word of a lie, he was looking at me with a look on his face that said, "I have come to avenge the motorbike frog species of Lake Richmond. Legend of your fear and your dad's love of frog chasey has travelled this great southern land, and now I'm here to simply say, 'Whatcha gonna do 'bout it bitch?'" I swear, that is what his little froggy face said. Maybe not the speech about frog chasey – I ad libbed that bit – but definitely from the way he was sitting on the toilet, I think he could tell I was busting to pee. Maybe frogs can smell fear, I don't know. And his head tilted to the right slightly with the attitude of, "Hey, fuck you, lady".

Under normal circumstances, I would totally phone a friend to get rid of the frog.

Except this evening. I'd figured if they saw the size of this frog, they'd laugh. I mean, he was tiny. Tiny and powerful in how he wielded my phobia and fear together in my face like a pair of emotionally manipulative nunchucks. Little fucker.

I decided to ladyballs up and face my fear. Being 25 and living in North Queensland meant I had a very tiny bathroom attached to my laundry at the back of the house. The toilet was basically situated right next to the shower screen. You could touch the shower screen with your knee if you turned 15 degrees to reach something, it was that small.

Off to the kitchen I went to find a piece of newspaper. In my mind, I figured I would coax the froggy friend onto the newspaper. Because, you know, you can control frogs.

Like heck you can! I mean, I like surprises in life, but I like my amphibians with predictability... which is why I'm scared of them.

He had other ideas. I guess I could understand. If you were tiny and green, and you had sensitive skin and you saw a giant piece of paper that's going to suck any moisture out of you, and the paper is at least 500 times your size, you'd be thinking about a plan B, too.

In the blink of an eye, my tiny foe jumped from the toilet to the shower screen. I screamed. Loudly. I also jumped at the same time. My heart raced. I had not been this close to a frog on purpose ever! This is what facing fear physically felt like. My hands were trembling. I was at real risk of pissing myself – both out of fear and busting for the toilet – but I was starting my self-talk of "Be brave, Belle, be brave."

I stepped towards the shower screen, with the newspaper held between me and my short denim skirt.

The frog jumped.

Not onto the paper.

Onto my freaking leg! All hell broke loose. I started screaming like a toddler who has just had their ice-cream ripped out of their hand by their older sibling, bouncing up and down on the spot. The more I did this, the more the bloody frog started moving his little sucky foot pads up my thigh, causing an increase in screaming and jumping, still holding the newspaper and flapping it about like a one-winged seagull.

I shifted my commotion towards the back door, screaming, "GET OFF! GET OFF! GET OFF! GET OFF! GET OFF! GET OFF!" All the while this frog was hitching his way further up my leg.

Eventually, I pulled the back door open, still screaming. The frog finally flung himself into the green ferns at the back door.

I raced back into the toilet, relieved in more ways than one. Bloody frogs. I'm still scared of them, but hey – at least I tried, I told myself.

There is nothing wrong with asking for help. Screw feeling embarrassed about it. There is also nothing wrong with failing at overcoming a fear. Or failing in general. At the least, you'll be able to laugh. One day. After counselling. And maybe a sangria or 27.

So, having thought about what happened the last time I tried to overcome this, I'm very nervous about attempting to overcome my fear of frogs with our creature-loving friend. And on camera. Live.

Eek.

It's on the list, though, so I need to follow through.

For me to prep for this, I decided to create a little mantra for myself, inspired by none other than the president of the United States. Not Obama, no – he wouldn't be suitable for this. You know the one. The one with the tiny hands and the hair. And the love of walls. Trump has become my fear-breaking mindset guru.

Each time I thought about it during the lead-up to this event, I'd feel my heart race a little faster, my palms get a little clammier, and my pants get a little tighter from stress-eating cookies. I honestly thought fear would burn calories – my pants say otherwise.

I had to find a way to switch this fear-based mindset around and be brave.

There were a couple of goals I'd set myself for the Facebook Live:

1. Not accidentally throw the frog at the wall.
2. Not pee my pants on a live stream.
3. Not vomit.
4. Not drink any alcohol before the event because I believe in facing my fears head on, and not numbing down dramas.
5. Successfully hold a frog for the first time in my life and NOT DIE!!!

I can generally summon a switch to focus like a laser beam when I want to achieve anything work-related. This was different. I needed to tap into my creativity and find some of those mindset tools I like to use.

One of my favourites is putting paralysing problems on a scale of 1–100 and finding something worse to help shift me forward. I had to come up with something which, experientially, would be worse than touching or holding a frog. I needed something a little quirky and not over-the-top dramatic like, say, losing a loved one. I've lost a few – I don't like going there, it makes me ugly cry on tap.

I started to forage through my brain looking for things where overcoming my fear of frogs would be the better option if my life depended on it.

Enter Donald Trump.

Now, I'm sure if Donald Trump is scared of frogs, he'd probably rather touch a frog than kiss me (note: not an invitation).

This is how I created the switch in mindset. I started asking myself the question, 'Would I rather kiss Donald Trump or be brave and touch a frog?'

Fair to say, I'm a highly visual person and hands down, every time I imagined the Trumpnado face comin' at me, the frog experience looked like a better option. Can you relate?

As we get further into the show, no amount of deep yogic breathing is going to cut it. I try to channel my inner Miyagi, my inner Yoda – but all of my inner mindset masters just don't cut it.

I even have a freak-out when they just try to get me to hold some squidgy moss. What's a mother to do but visualise the alternate option? The frog is not Donald Trump.

After holding snakes, seeing scorpions – not allowed to hold those, though – turtles and lizards, out comes Prince the majestic tree frog. I freak out before finding my centre with a chant of, "This is better than kissing Donald Trump."

I manage to hold the frog.

It's completely different to what I thought it would feel like. I pictured something cold, slimy and wet. You know when you go sit at a café, and some dirty grot has stuck a piece of chewed gum underneath the table, and it's started to dry, but not quite, and you accidentally touch it? That is what frogs feel like. A partially dried, chewed-up piece of gum. Sticky and gross.

Would I say fear faced? Yes. Fear gone? No. I won't actively go and pick up a frog, but I don't think I will (a) run away and lock myself in the bathroom, or (b) try to handle the problem myself unless I really, really have to. Read: I am the last person on the planet to remove a frog from the toilet.

That's one tiny act of attempted bravery off the list. Lauren still needs to hold Cuddles the tarantula, but we will save that for another day.

As filming wraps, we sit and have wine. Talk turns to parenting, and where Hector is at. Looks like the beautiful Lauren thought my co-parenting might be helpful to Hector.

I immediately decide to adopt Hector as my faux bro, or FB for short, to help him through the minefield that is co-parenting. It's pretty raw for him, so I can only share what has helped, and what has not helped, and offer to be his fauxmily given his blood support network is in New Zealand. Hector and I organise to catch up in May to chat about the single parent space. Appropriate considering Mother's Day is when it all unfolded three years ago anyway.

5

MAY

I'm more than happy to ask FB to come surfing, because he is in my friendzone – I don't have a crush on him, so it's easy. He declines. I head out after the Thursday morning school drop-off with my second-hand board and my wetsuit that I have purchased from Surf Dundee to catch a few nice little waves before I catch up with Hector later in the day.

The sand is cool. The water is warmer than the air. I pass some of the guys who are returning to the car park with their boards, giving a few "hello" and "have a good surf" pleasantries.

Spending time out on the water helps me gather my thoughts and think about what I can share with FB. I mean, I have a HUGE amount of empathy for single parents – especially dads.

Even just sitting out here amongst the waves, amongst this space, seems to create space. It's very zen. Okay, let's be real, I am in waist-deep water as it makes catching beginner waves easier, so technically I'm standing as I haven't mastered sitting on my board without it flipping me like a pancake yet – but still, zen.

Careful not to 'flop on my board like a wet fish', I have Surf Dundee's voice ringing in my head as I position my board, ready to make my mark, and catch the first little wave in, managing to get up – internal *woohoo, yay me*, no matter my form – before heading back out.

Seeing all the other middle-aged dad surfers sees my thoughts return to my own dad. Specifically, a decision that was made by my mum to move us far away from him for two years. Understanding if it was because of my failure to speak up about a long-held secret is on my bravery list – it's a big conversation to have with my last remaining parental figure, Hamish. It's something that needs to be put to rest.

Paddling out, I wait to catch another wave. I have improved but I still feel like a fake. Like my softboard – not a 'real' board. Like I shouldn't be here. It's not like swimming laps in a pool where there is a slow lane and a fast lane, and you can choose based on your skill. The green lady just don't roll that way. I do feel like the green lady and I are starting to understand each other a little more. She's very much like my life in general.

The next wave sees me return to thinking on my own parents, and how they influenced my own co-parenting situation.

In some ways, I'm very lucky that I grew up with parents who hated each other. I mean, they really, really hated each other.

It helped me find my voice as a tween and tell them that I loved them both, but that my role was not to be their pawn, to listen to how much each other was a horrible person between the drinking, the cheating and the wrongdoings they committed towards each other. That I loved them for being Mum and Dad.

It didn't change the fact that Dad still wouldn't set foot inside her house, or that high-school graduation caused great stress as I tried to keep them separated because their hatred of each other was greater than their love for me. That's my truth, anyway.

It did help me work out what I did not want for Abby and Bear. It helped me and their dad keep our pact to co-parent with kindness, and back each other on the important fronts.

It also helped me understand that quality time, not quantity time, mattered when it came to parenting, as I thought about the time I spent with my dad, the magic-maker.

My dad had this saying when I was growing up that stayed with me. He would say, "It's quality, not quantity, Belinda." I hated being called Belinda. It made me feel like I was in trouble. I'd look at him, at his dark, olive skin, his jet-black hair, his beer gut, his eyes that could either spark with mischief or darken with a storm of pain when it came time for us to leave. I always, always thought he was talking about my love of Kmart versus his love of David Jones (back then it was Aherns in Perth) when he said that.

My dad died when I was 29.

My dad was not perfect. Like all of us, he was flawed. He drank. He smoked. I chopped up more cartons of Benson & Hedges than you could count in a bid to stop him smoking, and he never told me off. He was never hurt by that action.

He was, however, very hurt by the actions of my mum. And sometimes, a dark cloud would cross the dry humour-filled facial landscape of the happy man and that hurt would seep out on a Sunday afternoon.

Generally, it would start to seep before we were shuffled back home in the post-divorce, second-hand red Kingswood.

Yep. We were an every-second-weekend deal. From the age of somewhere between five and six, "See you every day, Dad!" became "See you every second weekend, Dad". Reasons that a somewhere-between-five-and-six-year-old didn't quite get. During this painful transition, something else happened when he became every-second-weekend Dad. I didn't understand it. But I loved him for it. I still do, even though he is no longer here.

You see, my dad was magic.

I didn't know how to tell him at the time that he was, but he was. It took me until early adulthood to figure out he was magic. Nath (the father of my kids) is a good guy in the dad department. He's good at the silliness, and the sports, and creating magic, too. Anyway, that magic grew in my heart and mind. That love of adventure and wonder of the world grew slowly with that every-second-weekend love.

Picture this: a mid-thirties man goes to a children's park on the foreshore. He's not very fit. He has a beer gut, wears ill-fitting beige trousers and a shirt. He climbs a pole that has a large round ball on top and a bell inside. It's probably about 10 metres high, maybe 15. He hides two Mars Bars inside. This is probably at 6:30 am. He then hops back in his post-divorce, second-hand, red Kingswood wagon and drives 30 minutes to pick up his somewhere-between-five-and-six-year-old and her younger sister.

He then takes his somewhere-between-five-and-six-year-old and her younger sister to the park and suggests climbing the bell to see if they can ring it. It's quite a feat, but with a bit of a helping hand from dad, they both make it to the top.

Bingo! Out pops a Mars Bar!

"How did that get there?"

"Don't know," he replies, "must be magic."

We'd oooh and ahhh and wonder why other kids didn't know about this magic at the park.

The adventures would continue. Getting lost on some road trip. Making an '80s version of a podcast where Dad would pretend to be a mad dentist with an electric can opener and a tape recorder. Jumping off a certain hill out at Point Peron, or skipping out of the bushes at a park at certain times of the year – an annual event that went well into my teen years and became kinda embarrassing – only to discover he was secretly making a time lapse video of us growing up.

All these little things, based on quality time over quantity. All these little things; seeds planted long ago that had the chance to grow into beauty.

The life lesson which, when I look back, reminds me constantly to look for and cherish the good in people – as flawed as that may be, as it's not free of hurt – over constantly looking at their flaws and faults.

We all make mistakes. Sometimes the dream doesn't work out. Mine didn't. But, as my daughter pointed out on her little quote jar, "Just because the past didn't work out how you wanted, doesn't mean the future can't be more than you imagine." She's a wise kid. My dad would have loved her. Luckily, her dad does.

I know the post-divorce war territory from a child's perspective. Peace is better than persecution, from either side.

Partnering is different to parenting.

If the partnership – for whatever reason – didn't work, it does not make either of you a bad person for the rest of your life. It does not preclude you, or me, from deserving happiness. It certainly does not make you a bad father. So, please, hold on to the good guy that you are.

My dad was right. It's quality, not quantity, that matters.

I start to think of what Hector and I might talk about, and I think of what I can use to lighten the conversation while still being real and brave and sharing what it was actually like to go through divorce. To lose yourself, and then work to find yourself again. To realise that you might have conversations about things you won't always be ready for. To know that your kids are resilient and will be okay.

I catch my last wave for the morning, quietly high-fiving myself on the inside for standing up on my board a lot more than I have previously, and because I'm just loving being out amongst it. Heading back up to the car park, I give the surfers that are now heading out a "nice morning for it" as I pack up and go home.

Hector and I meet at a café in the city. He is delivering some bearded dragons to a customer in Scarborough, so it makes sense to meet at Gordon St Garage for lunch and chats. It's become a bit of a regular haunt for me while Abby is at ballet, my place to meet coaching clients in the city, or to work on workshop stuff. A mixture of tables and booths, big glass windows, great light, good coffee and enough noise to have a private conversation.

I watch Hector walk in. He really is tall. Lumberjacky in build, even, I think. Wearing his 'Beasties as Buddies' khakis and rust-brown Blundstones, he stands out from the petrol-blue business suits and crisp white shirts with black, polished Florsheim shoes. Hector looks like he doesn't care and isn't fazed at all.

As he approaches and sits at the table, I can see the sadness in his face. Guess he hasn't digested the sad Care Bear yet. I know that feeling, though. It's the feeling like you have failed your kids, and your idea of success as a family.

"Hey, Belle," Hector greets me. "Hit me with your advice, and some funny stories if you've got them. I need to know there's a light through this, 'cause it's feelin' pretty dark right now."

The sadness is in his voice, too.

"Oh, Hector. I get it. I have been in your shoes. But with heels. My best piece of advice? Practise being kind to yourself."

"What was it like, I mean, can you talk me through it?"

"Where do you want me to start? With the end, the fun that is co-parenting, how to get some self-love happening, or the awkward conversation I've just recently had with my kids about dating?"

"Talk me through how it ended, if you are okay to do that, and how you navigate the whole single parent and business thing, and when you get back to feeling like you again."

"Okay. Let's start with the end that was the beginning, or the beginning of the ending. They overlap, so I'll start with how it all broke down. Our kids are the same age, right?"

"Yeah, they are pretty close."

I pause and look at my kale salad that has just turned up before launching into my story.

"Do you know the book *Eat Pray Love* by Elizabeth Gilbert? The movie has Julia Roberts in it."

"I haven't seen the movie, Belle, or read the book – I'm more of a nature documentary person, in case you couldn't guess. Not really a chick-flick guy."

Eat Pray Love was one of those books that when my relationship was turning to shit, I'd lie huddled as far over on the right side of the bed as I could, silently crying at the unhappiness in my life, and I'd think of Liz Gilbert on her bathroom floor.

I couldn't really ask God for an answer or anything, because, well, I hadn't fully made peace with Him yet. I would ask the universe. Deep down, I probably meant God, but I'd been at war with Him since my mum died. So I would lie there, in a concoction of flannel pyjamas and misery, waiting for Bear who was then three years old to have night terrors once again, and wonder, *What would Liz do?*

I couldn't just up and go off eating pizza, hanging out at ashrams and talking to wise old toothless Balinese men. I mean, I could, but I chose not to. I had kids. I had a business. I had debts. I had a relationship that, like Liz Gilbert, was not where I thought it should be.

One night, as I lay there so far over on the edge I'm sure my feet were poking out the side, ready to move to the couch at any minute, I changed the question. I started asking myself, *What would I do?*

I had bought so much into the fact that success, for me, meant giving my kids two parents who were together until the end, because of how much I did not want them to have divorced parents. I completely overlooked all the other stuff that might be more important to teach kids.

What would Belle do? became the midnight thought that had me paralysed on the pillow with silent tears running down my cheeks as I listened to the kids' dad breathe like a Darth Vader–coffee percolator hybrid. He slept, while I resented his sleeping.

Belle didn't know what the heck to do. She just knew that the unhappiness was seeping in everywhere.

There had been no cheating, no affairs. Just a big mismatch in defining values and in our definitions of happiness. In what priorities contributed to it, and what ones took it away.

I'd crafted this whole story about success and happiness. If I was successful, then I'd be happy. Success meant a family unit that stayed together. Success meant earning six figures. Success meant a four-bedroom, two-bathroom house – that good suburban wife tick of approval. Except that was not my definition of success. That was me trying to fit someone else's definition of success. Mine is split between two locations. Location one: a converted warehouse-style apartment with big windows for light, storage for bikes, surfboards and paddleboards, and access to the beach and parks. Location two: a small, sustainable, off-the-grid cottage and hobby farm near the coast. Suburbia was never on my list.

The family unit that stayed together, though – that was a big one. Come from a broken home, and at a very young age you start telling yourself a story that your friends who have a mum and a dad together are better off than your family. Try drawing a family tree that looks more like a sketch of the powerlines on Patong Beach in Thailand, and you, too, would wish for a simplistic family unit where you don't have to explain half-brothers and sisters, third marriages, and wonder whether Dad's current fiancée should be included. Worst high-school assignment ever.

Success meant working so hard at everything, trying to hold this image together. This image that, if you stripped back the social filters and public photoshopping, you would quickly realise may not be a picture of success, and maybe success would be better off measured in feeling as opposed to being measured in time, or things, or money, or structure.

So while on paper everything looked successful, I was – or we were – unhappy. Deeply unhappy.

The question got louder each time I would lie on the edge of the bed. *What would I do?*

How long could I try to fix something that was broken? What was I actually teaching my kids about life? About success? About happiness? That they should stay even if they were the cost?

I thought about this so much, until one day I got my answer and I realised that I had to change my attachment to the idea of success and happiness being structural. That I'd gotten the story all wrong.

Happiness is not structural. A happy family is not structural. A happy family, or happiness, is emotional. We had to change the structure.

Like any restructure I had seen in corporate, there is always a tipping point. The same happened in our family. One day – Mother's Day in 2015, actually – we reached ours, and life as we knew it imploded.

It came back to what we wanted to teach the kids about happiness. What space did we want for them? What was their experience to be like? Maybe, just maybe, it was possible that we could still teach them all these things – it just wouldn't happen under the same roof.

"So what happened when you were no longer under the same roof?" Hector asks.

"That was a tough and emotional day. Not in the way that I expected, though."

When I got the kids home to our rental house one day, and their dad was no longer there, there was a huge sense of feeling like I had irrevocably failed my family. That picture was now in its raw, unedited, emotional state. No more hiding.

I sat slumped on the edge of the bed, staring into the walk-in wardrobe that quite clearly said 'it is done'. I had to tell both kids that Dad would not be home. That it was not their fault. That even though we all knew the day was coming, I was so sorry it was there. That we both loved them.

I cried. In front of my kids. Never had I felt like I had failed them more. I cried for my kids. For myself. For the definition that I had just killed so that a new one – a healthier one – could grow in its place. Bear didn't really understand what was going on.

This was the first time my kids ever saw me as vulnerable. Bear doesn't remember it.

What my daughter did next, though, would be one of the stand-out moments of kindness in my life until the day I die.

I sat there crying. Crying for failing them structurally, for not delivering what I had wanted so badly as a kid myself. My first-grade daughter disappeared into her room, coming back with a gift all wrapped up.

"Here, Mum. I was saving this to give to you when we move into our new house. But I think I should give it to you today."

As I unwrapped the present I saw the back of a photo frame and, flipping it over, a colouring-in page that she had cut out and placed in the brown wooden frame. You could see that it had been cut out by a seven-year-old. The edges were jagged, the brown cardboard of the backing of the photo frame exposed on the left side. The frame was too big for her craft work, but it was the contents of the picture that got me.

Amidst orange, green, blue, red, purple and yellow swirls and hearts, she had coloured in the word PEACE.

"Oh, Abby. I love you. It's beautiful."

Cue more tears, the ugly crying kind. Because to be seen – fully seen by another human being, with all your vulnerability, all your strength, all your flaws – and still be loved, that is a rare and beautiful gift. It made me realise just how much my daughter was seeing.

I just hope that my kids grow up to realise that leaving a situation filled with sadness and unhappiness is not failing, it might just be succeeding in the best possible way.

"So how do you guys co-parent?"

"Well, I am proud that it is done in a way where the kids are considered first. That this redefining of our family was done in such a way that our kids do not become pawns in the parental game of emotional chess. We still have conversations together about their education, or eating vegetables or not eating vegetables, and homework. We still do things together – for now, given neither of us have a partner – like take them to the movies. We are going to see *Jumanji* on the weekend.

"How did you turn your light back on, Belle?"

"That is more of a turn-on, turn-off, turn-on-again process. I think you work on one part, and then when you think you have it down pat, you work on another. Change takes time. But I think being kind to yourself is really, really important. Self-care.

"Practising being kind to yourself, when you haven't done it for quite some time, and when you feel immense guilt over things not working out, and when you are blaming yourself for tearing apart a definition that you have held onto for practically your whole entire life, well, basically it feels like you are trying to learn Chinese when you have no idea how to even say hello. Totally foreign, weird, stupid, dumb, embarrassing.

"Do you really want to know what I did? Because it's embarrassing for me to tell you, but if it helps, I'm happy to."

"I'm all ears, Belle."

"Well, I'd first caught sight of the person I really didn't recognise after moving into the new house with the kids as a single parent. I was shocked. Not at the state of my hair or anything, although that was pretty bad. Not at what I was wearing – that was pretty bad, too. I looked older than I was. Waaay older. I had been avoiding mirrors for as long as I could remember while my loathing of my own body grew as I struggled to accept the post-baby body, even four years on post-baby. I'd loved on everyone else, but hated on myself.

"So when I finally stopped and stared back at my reflection, and actually looked into my own eyes, well, it was my eyes. But there was no spark. They looked sad, and a little bit dead. It's a sadness I can recognise in others now when they are going through internal battles around what the right thing to do is, without thinking about the cost to themselves."

Hector looks down, and then back up. I can see he gets it.

"Well, now that I had done what Belle would do, I was left alone with two kids, staring into a mirror, asking whether I would love me. Talk about hard conversations.

"I decided to commit to me for three months, which probably turned into a lot longer, really, given I'm still not back out there dating. I thought I'd try to love me and heal me before I put myself back out there. You know, in man land. I wanted me to be good with me. I mean, if I thought forward, one day my kids would grow and leave home, and it would just be me. One day I might be lucky enough to be the active, hot old lady with grey hair who had lived the shit out of life, who was farewelling people she loved, and it would just be me. And maybe apartment cats. Hopefully not apartment cats. Can you imagine death by apartment cats?"

"Not really – they kill a lot of native animals. Not a cat fan, to be honest, Belle."

"Right, well, I wanted to be okay with just me. I mean, me and the kids. I mean, I wanted the kids to love themselves, too, but it's hard to teach acceptance of yourself to others if you don't do it yourself, right?"

"So what'd you do? What was your process?"

"I wrote on my ensuite mirror in whiteboard marker: 'Find something nice to say.' I also bought a treadmill and found a PT – my friend Becs – to help me train. She refers to that period of my life as 'squirrel cheeks'. I'm kinda back there at the moment, but I'm working on fixing that. Intention still needs action, right?"

"Ah, yep," Hector says, "nothing changes if nothing changes. That's true."

"So, day one, I stared at my eyes. They really looked hollow and lifeless. I didn't know what to say. It felt like the time I had to tell a cowboy I dated in Queensland that, no, I wasn't looking for the ranch wife life, and I was catching a plane to London in three days. Uncomfortable. Uncomfortable and weird. Except this time, the sad eyes were mine."

"I think I have those right now," Hector says.

I smile back at him, giving an understanding wink. "You'll get through this. I promise."

"I hope so, Belle. I hope so. Anyway, what did you say?"

"Well, I searched for something, anything, that I could say to start being kind to myself. Maybe even to forgive myself for failing.

"As I stared, I came up with the comment: 'you have hair'. My hair wasn't great. It certainly wasn't the long, sun-kissed brunette hair of the adventurer that I knew. The well-kept, loved hair that would take my hairdresser an hour to style at the end because there was so much of it. I had, as I was prone to do when life was not going great, chopped it all off in a bid to create someone else instead. Except the last big chop I gave it, I went all-in. Gone were the long locks, replaced by a short, bleached blonde, Gwyneth-Paltrow-in-*Sliding-Doors*-type style.

"Except, Hector, I was no Gwyn. The regrowth had me constantly feeling like I had Mediterranean leg stubble growing out of my head. It was a good vision in theory, but did not work. I also had my daughter question why I cut my hair off like the old ladies that she saw. Anyway, I digress.

"I don't want to be the old lady with short hair because she thinks long hair is no longer age-appropriate, so relents to daggying on down. Lets the body go. Lets the style go. Lets the light go. For no reason at all except to do what she thinks she was supposed to do, or was conditioned to believe she should do.

"I'd been growing it back out. It takes me roughly four years to go from super-short to bra-length tresses again. Except at this stage, I was mid-length and feeling daggy.

"So there I stood, looking in the mirror, starting with 'I had hair'. It was the best I could come up with. I looked at my body and saw one that did not belong to the adventurer. I hated it, so I decided to start at the top, with the hair."

"Well, Belle, I don't know if that one will help me, 'cause, uh, as you can see, I don't have a lot of hair."

"Whoops, sorry. Good thing about hair – for me, anyway – is that if you cut it, it grows back. Anyway, each day I started this kindness ritual, building on the day before, practising kindness to myself, as weird as it was.

"I have hair and it's growing – tick – you can skip that one hahaha.

"I have eyes and I can see beauty in this world – tick.

"I have teeth and they look great when I smile – tick.

"I have skin that is in good condition for my age – tick.

"This practice went on for days. Days to weeks. Weeks to months. As I continued down my body, I found ways to love my arms, my shoulders… because of the purpose they have."

"Did you struggle with anything?"

"Yes. I struggled with my stomach. If I'm being honest, I still do. It was the most changed after having kids, and it became the most loathed. It basically looks like a cat went to town on a scratching post, leaving a trail of destruction – stretch marks from carrying babies and a non-cancerous growth, which basically made it the equivalent of carrying twins twice. Seeing as we are sharing stuff, it is my biggest fear for men to see my stomach, if and when I get back out there dating."

"Look, Belle, as a friend, that's not an issue. From what I know, you are an awesome lady and the right guy will see how awesome you are. Sounds like you have been doing a good job at being kind to yourself, though."

"Well, I guess I have learnt the importance of belief from the workshops I do, and I see what happens when someone believes in you.

"Belief is, by far, the most important thing in the world. Believing good things about yourself, and what you deserve and are worthy of, is by far the most challenging thing to cultivate, only because of how foreign it can feel if you haven't learnt it.

"When it came to looking at my stomach, the truth is, I couldn't love it. I couldn't accept it. It was so changed from the body of the adventurer, the triathlete, the body that I had worked so hard for in the first place, I couldn't stand to look at it, despite the magnificent feats it had performed.

"I bypassed it. I placed it in the too-hard basket, and while I worked on bringing the light back into my eyes and my soul, I could not stand the sight of myself between my boobs and my butt. It was yet another death that I didn't acknowledge. Outside of my control.

"I left that area, hiding it with shame instead of looking at it with pride for its capabilities and power. I refused to love it."

"You're right, Belle. People talk about self-love like it's an easy thing to do."

"That's the thing about easy, though – you look at things like stand-up paddleboarding, or surfing, or anything else that someone has had time to practice with ease and flow, and think it will be easy, only it's not. It can be hard, and it takes time.

"So I guess that forgiving yourself, or your life, your experience – whatever – whether it is something you had control over or whether it is something outside of your control that you still feel a debt to, that takes practise. I started with the little things. But the stomach – that was a big thing. That was the whole reason I wanted to do a bikini comp. I thought if

I could get myself to a place where I was 'stage ready' and put everything out in public, that I would then love all of the outside unconditionally. I'd get comfortable in my discomfort.

"Moving through the discomfort zone gets a little easier day by day. Life will return, buddy. Laughter will come back, and acceptance becomes easier. Sooo... That was heavier than a 400g steak and a Guinness!"

"I really appreciate it, though," Hector says. "Thanks for sharing."

"You are welcome. How about I tell you a funny story instead? Because, depending on parenting arrangements, you may end up having some conversations that you just aren't prepared for. Outside of the frogs and stuff, do you have, you know, a 'normal' pet?"

"Nope. No pets."

"Well, I thought it would be a good idea to get a dog. I guess you could call her the dog of divorce. We – the kids and I – actually, mainly I – decided to get a French bulldog. A female dog. Me thinking that I would avoid the whole leg-humping, stuffed toy-humping, rug-humping, anything-humpable-humping explaining to the kids. There was already enough to work on with the move, the resettling of the family, and turning some lights back on where self-love was concerned.

"I wasn't sure if I was up for explaining birds and bees single-handedly to the kids. At least, not after explaining that Mum and Dad were not going to be living together anymore.

"But, as is the case in life, there are few things that you can control, or try to control. Knowing what your dog is going to be like is not one of them...

"Before my friend, Jo, who lives in Tasmania, left for her wild life amongst chooks, oysters and firewood, she gifted my son a large, green T-rex stuffed toy as a birthday present. Bear, my son, and Claire, her daughter had become fast friends on adventures to the zoo and museum, and shared a love of talking and hiding amongst the trees in parks. The dinosaur was meant to be a present to remind Bear of their friendship.

"Giant and green, T-Bone, as he was named, was too big to fit on the bed, so he would sit on the floor where he doubled as a beanbag. Perfect for a little boy who likes routine and consistency, has just turned four, and has had his world turned upside down with a new house and new way of his mum and dad being in his life.

"Until Fry.

"I swear when my dog looks at me, she is looking at me with the disgust of a French food critic who has just found pubic hair in the soufflé. I always imagine her internal monologue – in French. *'Allo, Belle! I see zat yeu ev not spent enuf time wiz me. I am zerefore go-een tue sheet on yur cah-pet and chew yur last four undred doolear Leona Edmiston shuz from yur old life so yeu ev nuh-zeeng but fleep-flups.'*"

Hector laughs at my terrible French accent as coffees arrive at our table.

"Our dog is small in size for a Frenchie, but big in personality. She is a fan of revenge shits on carpets, stealing stationery and gutting stuffed toys like they are fish, leaving around the house a trail of fluffy carcasses and devastated kids who still can't learn to put their stuff away. You'd think that after the massacre of 12 Ty beanies in the spring of 2015, they'd learn. Nope. Tradesmen even have to be warned not to leave screwdrivers and monkey wrenches on the ground, as anything is fair game. They look at me like, 'Yeah, lady, like a dog will steal my tools – never happened before,' until they reach for their Phillips head, only to spot the nine-kilo klepto wielding it in her mouth as though she is smoking a 1920s cigarette in the streets of Paris.

"*'Whet eh yeu looking et, treddie? Deed no whun tell yeu zet I smoke pheeleeps eds? Zat wood be teepical uv my own-eh. She left me ellone fuh five meenots, so I em revenge smoh-keeen ur screw driverrr.'*

"I try to warn people that her looks are deceiving. Behind the squished-in face of cuteness is a dog with a real dark side. Including what she does to poor Mr T-Bone. I honestly had never met a female humper of a dog before. So when Fry eventually stumbled across stuffed toy gold, we had a problem. Well, I had a problem."

———

"Muuum! What is Fry doing to Mr T-Bone?" My son had a confused look on his face. "It looks like she is trying to go for a piggyback, or playing horsey, but I'm not sure."

Abby piped up, "Yeah, mum, what is she doing… haha?" She raised her eyebrows, thinking that she might know something her little brother did not yet know. I could see her waiting to pounce towards my ear.

As I looked at Fry getting her lady boner on with Mr T-Bone, I had the realisation that there were going to be other questions that I might have to handle. Alone. Life really is like that. Most things are out of our control. Tell the age-appropriate truth? Avoid? Normalise sex? How much of a parenting conversation did I need to have right now?

"Well, I think Fry is trying to have a special dance with Mr T-Bone, Bear. But dogs don't really know how to dance, so this is her best move!"

Abby raced over, her eyes wide, and I could see her mischievous knowing dancing across her face – the look she gets when she thinks she has stumbled across a secret chocolate stash that no one else in the house knows about.

She whispered, "I know – she's trying to have S-E-X!!!"

"Abby, how do you know?"

"*Animal Planet*!!! I've seen all sorts of animals have S-E-X!" She collapsed into silent giggles. "But she isn't going to make any babies with Mr T-Bone!"

"Aw, Belle, that's classic. I've got one of each too, so I'm sure I might have to have conversations with my daughter about girl stuff."

"Well, I never grew up with a brother. For the most part, my only experience with a brother-type person was my neighbour who pulled a bit of 'you show me yours and I'll show you mine' when I was about four years old.

"Being the kid that was into exploring and dares and whatnot, of course I decided he should go first. I had no idea what I was going to see. My poor friend obliged, dropping his pants, only to have me go running like a dibber-dobber, screaming down the green shag pile carpet to my parents about the innocent four-year-old penis I had just witnessed in our hallway.

"Having a son, though, well that is a learning curve in itself. I had thought I was getting a rough-and-tumble, do-now-ask-questions-later little boy. And for some things, he was very much a 'hey, screw you, Mumma, I'm going to streak naked in the supermarket/play-ground/street/beach/train'-type little person.

"I'd also never really thought too much about how I would parent a little boy the majority of the time and deal with penises, or other body parts, thinking that his dad would still handle those types of conversations.

"This gift of a little boy has been instrumental in getting me to practise my game face with conversations and situations that I am not necessarily ready for. He has been some of the best training in being brave and creating safe spaces for others. He has pushed me to break stereotypes and filters I have created in spaces where I really know nothing."

"What do you mean?" Hector asks.

"Well, as a single mum, I am conscious that I need to double hat and be able to do what might be traditionally seen as 'boy stuff' and also 'girl stuff'. A lot of the stuff, I never had the opportunity to do. So, while I'm all for adventures and am great at taking my kids to foreign countries, up 58-metre fire lookout trees, and down caves, I have zero skills in kicking soccer balls, surfing, until just recently, or skateboarding, and don't really know anything about surf or skate culture except that teenage nerd me made the assumption that they must be heavily connected with pot-smoking, dreadlock-wearing dudes.

"He's been great at opening up my blind spots and pointing out that I don't know what I don't know. Without saying a word."

"Such as?"

"Well, when your five-year-old decides to say to you, 'Watch out for that string, it's going to hit you in the nuts', you soon realise that you might be having conversations about the things he doesn't know about as yet."

"Okay, this should be good."

"Picture this: Bear and I are standing together in the garage, packing boogie boards in the boot to head to the surf beach. I'd made an ill MacGyver attempt at a marker for where to stop the car in the garage, in the form of a string hanging down from the garage-door-tracky thingy so I didn't hit a wall. Anyway, it swung towards me as I opened the boot.

"It's completely useless, except to remind me that I am not handy, and there are traditional man-fix-it-type skills that I do not yet have.

"As I looked at my little boy, it dawned on me that this co-parenting gig was going to see me handle some conversations that I had just assumed would be directed at his dad. Yet here I was. About to explain to a five-year-old that, 1. Your nuts are not on your face, and 2. I don't have nuts, and 3. What they are actually called, and where they are.

"'Bear, where do you think your nuts are?'

"'In your face? I don't know! It's just I hear people say they get it in the nuts, so I thought it was like in your body.'

"'No, darling. Mummy doesn't have nuts. What you are talking about is the place just behind your penis, and mummy doesn't have a penis.'

"'Isn't that all called my penis?'

"'Well, darling boy, those are called your testicles.'

"'You mean I have tentacles like an octopus? Yay! I'm an octopus.'

"'No, the word is testicles. Octopuses have tentacles. Another word is nuts. Or balls. Or family jewels.'

"'You mean I have jewels in my body? How did they get there?'

"'Oh, you were born with them, Bear.'"

Hector laughs. "OMG, so funny. Don't you love kids?"

"Yeah, they are pretty good. Look, I know I'm lucky on the co-parent front – it's why things like going to *Jumanji* happen. Don't get me wrong, there are things we still find annoying about each other, and at the very start it was really hard. We just try to keep the kids front and centre and focus on what each other is good at. He's good at sport stuff. I'm good at conversations about penises, as it turns out. We both have our strengths and shortcomings. Kids will see it all eventually. Just be the best you."

"Thanks so much, Belle. It's been great getting some perspective."

"Hey, when you are ready, maybe we can tackle the whole single space together. I'm sure I might need to call upon you for a guy's perspective, because, my friend, the last date I had was a Medjool, and if I don't do something about it, I'll be looking like one before I get back out there."

The weekend passes by, Monday rolls around, and so does one of my regular check-ins with Jo.

"Jo, what is that on your head? Hey, I've got a funny story to tell you!"

"It's a muff, I own about four of them. Got into wearing them when I lived in Scotland. Why? What's up? How's the surfing going? You getting fitter?"

"Muff! You are wearing a muff on your head! Bahahaha. OMG, that is too funny. I'm so immature. Um, yeah – all good. Surf is getting better... I'm still a bit rubbish, but anyway, it's more a mental battle now. Why are you so rugged up? It's still warm here, we are having a late summer!"

"Yeah, it's almost like year-round winter. It's fucking cold. Okay, shoot. Make me laugh. And then I've got news for you, too."

"Well, you know the whole co-parenting thing, and how sometimes we have dinner with the kids together or go see a movie with them?"

"Yeah – I think that is weird, but anyway, go on."

"Well, I had a realisation that I am highly likely to be the one having the sex conversations not only with my daughter, but quite possibly with my son. I think I might be the more liberal parent."

"Why, what happened?"

"Well, we took the kids to see *Jumanji* – you know, the new one with Dwayne Johnson and Jack Black."

"Is it any good? I haven't seen it yet. The movies are like a two-hour drive from here and I can't be arsed."

"Jo. It was so funny. They made it more about going into a video game as opposed to a board game. Anyway, there is a girl who ends up in the body of Jack Black."

"Who's he? Oh, I know – he's the short, beardy, hairy dude. Go on."

"Well, there is a scene in the movie, where the girl (Jack Black) has a crush on one of the other characters (also a guy), and has to give him mouth-to-mouth."

"And???"

"Jack Black's character gets an erection and starts freaking out about the peen having a mind of its own. There is a pants shot, so of course the cinema erupts in laughter. The kids are like, 'What's so funny? What's so funny?' Their dad is all... 'Ummm, I don't know, not sure, don't get it.'"

"Oh, right, so then what happened?"

"Well, Abby leans over to Bear and says, 'Don't worry, Mum will tell us after, we'll find out.'"

"Because you are the parent that is in charge of that stuff?"

"Yep. I'm the one who says vagina and penis, and talks about poo and periods and stuff. I'm pretty calm with it, even though it seems odd to be talking to the kids about it – I don't want them to have any hang-ups. I think I find it easier.

"So as soon as we leave the movies, the kids and I get in the car, and I had completely forgotten about the erection scene, when Abby decides to pipe up with, 'Mum, are you going to tell us now?'

"'Tell you what?' I say.

"'You know – about the pants! What was so funny about the pants?'"

Jo starts laughing. "I don't have to deal with that yet with Claire, but thanks for the heads-up in case we see *Jumanji*. So what did you do?"

"Well, I mustered my calm, and said, 'Okay, well, you know how the girl was in the guy's body?'

"And the kids go 'yeah'.

"'And you know how she kissed the other guy to bring him back to life?'

"'Yeah,' the kids say again.

"I glance at them in the rearview mirror, seeing that they think they are about to find out the secret location of Santa's warehouse. Their eyes are wide in anticipation. So funny.

"Well, anyway, sometimes when boys kiss girls, or something nice happens to them, they can't control their penises and they go hard. They get what's called an erection."

"And what did the kids do?"

"Well, this is where it gets funny. Bear bursts out laughing and says, 'THAT HAPPENS TO ME SOMETIMES! HOW COULD DAD NOT KNOW ABOUT ERECTIONS – HE HAS A PENIS!!!'"

Jo and I are now in fits of laughter.

"Oh, my God. That's fucking funny. Well, I guess we know who's going to be having the sex talks and puberty talks with the kids then. How did you handle that comment? Hahaha, that's just gold."

"Well, I wanted to make sure their dad came out of it okay, and explained that Dad is really good at soccer and explaining rules in AFL and knows lots about skiing, and he might just find these types of chats harder than Mum."

"Hahaha. So, tell me, have you been brave with this chap yet? You know, Hot Hands?"

"No, I'm still a big chickenshit. But I have been surfing, and I have been—"

"BelleBelleBelleBelle!" she cuts me off. "You are *not* being fucking brave. Have you booked in to see him?"

"No. Well, I don't want to. Last time it was all, 'Hey, so are you making space for someone?' and I'm all facedown on the table thinking like, *What the fuck? Do you ask everyone this, or just me?*"

"Why don't you ask him for a surf?"

"Because I don't know where he is at. My gut tells me he's got his own stuff going on, and I think I'll just leave it."

"That's stupid. You are being a bigger chicken than the ones I have running around the house! Anyway, you know what I think."

"Yep, I know. Look, it is a problem. He's really good at acupuncture, so if I do say something, and it's all embarrassing and I've made a dick of myself, then I have to find another acupuncturist, and I like our banter and chats. So I think I should just leave it in the friendzone."

"Okay, well keep me posted. Gotta bounce."

"Wait, wait, wait, wait! I want to hear your news! What's going on?"

"Oh, okay. Well, I think I have a girl crush, like a proper 'I think I might not just be straight' girl crush."

"Jo..."

"Yeah, what?"

"Well, it just makes wearing a muff on your head even funnier."

"Hahaha, I know. I hadn't thought of that. I'd wear this no matter what."

"Okay, do tell."

"When I was at high school, I used to really like this girl called Birdie, but I never really understood why. We'd leave little notes for each other in a downpipe on the side of the wall near the canteen. She was in her senior year, and I was two years down... I just idolised her and followed her around. Anyway, it's a long story, but she bought a puffy jacket off my friend through Gumtree. I thought I'd see if she remembered me."

My eyes go wide as I watch my bestie go all schoolgirl giggly in her tiny kitchen. She's kind of clapping her hands and swaying side to side. "Okay, keep going."

"Well, I'm trying to figure things out, but you are the first person I am sharing this with, so I'm kinda trying to work out if I might *like her* like her, and if she likes me too. Turns out she remembers me, so we are chatting online. I need to do some research. It might be why I've never felt quite right in my other relationships."

"Back the truck up, Jo. What kind of research?"

"Oh, you know, to see if I could be a lesbian, and if I could be a good lesbian. I can tell you about this because you and I always tell the truth and I know we will be good no matter what, and you are pretty openminded, so I feel safe processing this with you."

"Jo, you know I love you no matter what. I don't care if you are straight, gay, bi, non-binary, or whatever other term you can choose these days. I love you because you are Jo, and you are honest."

"That's why I'm telling you. Anyway, I'll keep you posted. But I'm going to go find out about how to be a good lesbian and see if I think I could do it. You're not the only person being brave and doing new things, by the looks of it."

"Well, that's not on my list. I'll stick with man land, thanks. I'm here for you, though."

"Okay, really gotta go. Hey, ask him for a surf. Before you fly out to Vegas."

She hangs up.

As always, Jo, my centre of truth and reflection, gets me to think about *why*. Why is this brave act of asking Baker for a surf so tricky for me? I mean, I've done lots of other cool stuff. I held a frog! I'm scared of those. But that was more phobia than fear.

I know why.

Fucking rejection. Fear of rejection is an arsehat. Feeling rejection, perceived or not, is like the arsehat sombrero of arsehats. You become totally shaded by it, blocking the sun and allowing darker thoughts to wash over you.

Two weeks before Lauren and I fly out for our Vegas-slash-Grand Canyon road trip, I figure I'll go and see Baker. It's been a month since I last saw him.

I go through the usual stress of 'Do I dress up or dress down?' 'Do I choose fancy boy-cut black lace knickers that have now been purchased, or do I stick with the best Bonds black undies?' I spend way too much time agonising over my undie choice for acupuncture.

Back I go to the light-filled studio near the beach, while my daughter is at ballet. As I walk in, Bakes pipes up with a "Hey, lesbo!" to break the ice. He's pretty good at putting me at ease.

I blush. "Stop it! It's not funny! I'm so embarrassed."

"Hahaha! What seems to be the problem?"

"Hamstring. Again. I've been surfing, and I'm flying out to the States tomorrow night with Lauren, so I want to make sure the back and legs are going to hold up okay for the Grand Canyon hike."

"Oh, right. Well, I'm glad you've come to see me! You know the drill, get undressed and get on the table, and I'll be back in when you're ready."

I oblige. Facedown in the hole on the table. I'm starting to like having my face wedged in the table hole. It is the perfect place to make a 'what the fuck' face without the face being seen. Bakes walks back in.

"So, you looking forward to the Grand Canyon?"

"Yes."

"And what are your sleeping arrangements again?"

"Lauren and I are sharing a bed."

"What if she actually really likes you and makes a move?"

"That won't happen. I'm not her type. What about you? Are you gay?"

I catch him off guard with the playful banter and watch through the hole in the table as his feet stop and his calf muscles tense up. He has quite nice legs. These conversations are so weird and awkward, as there are no facial expressions to read.

"No. Did you think I was gay?"

"Well, when I heard Becs talk about you, I thought that maybe you had to be, but I had never met you, so I didn't know. Everyone talked about you as one of the girls. I pictured you a bit different."

"And now?"

"Ummm, no. I don't think you are gay." *I think you are super-hot and adorable and funny and just wish I was more confident in my body as I'd want you to rip all my clothes off and just totally ravage me.* My thoughts are in overdrive. My date life is officially a drought. Three years now. It could have its own GoFundMe page with the hashtag #datedrought.

He says, "So, are you making space for your type, then?"

This is where the 'what the fuck' face comes in. *Why am I being asked these questions? I don't get it. Is it chit-chat, does he like me, does he ask everyone these types of questions?* I don't even know if I should ask Becs if this is the case.

"Ummm... why?"

"Just curious. That's all."

"Well, I'm feeling very vulnerable here. These are not easy conversations for me."

"Why? How are you vulnerable right now?"

"Are you kidding me? I'm lying facedown on a massage table in mum undies being asked questions by one of the cool people. It's much easier for me to talk to you when I'm looking at you."

"Hang on, I'm the one who should be feeling vulnerable."

"What do you mean? How can you be vulnerable? You are part of the cool crowd. I could hardly speak to you at the Gatsby event last year. I almost had a panic attack as I'm so not good at those dress-up scenarios. Plus, I can't see your facial expressions with my face stuck in a hole and needles stuck in my legs and back, so I'm pretty sure that I am vulnerable. I mean, you are the fully clothed, fully fit one."

I watch his feet pause at the top of the table. I know if I look up I'll be eyeballing his groin. I press my face into the massage table hole a little more, knowing I'll have a towel and circle imprint on my face once this is over. Please, God, make this be over.

"Well, I see you as someone who is accomplished and successful, so when we met at the Gatsby thing, *I* found it hard to talk to *you*. I mean, why would someone like you, who has their own business and has got it all sorted, want to talk to someone like me? You are the intimidating one."

My brain is going, *Are you fucking kidding me?*

"Are you kidding? How can I be intimidating? I am like the nerdy wallflower. Socially awkward and all."

"You remember *Melrose Place*? Well, I think of you like Amanda from D&D advertising."

"So you think of me like a cold-hearted corporate bitch? Great. Thanks." I am now wishing that there were no chats as I lay pretty much trapped on the table, unable to do anything but respond to personal questions, all the while needles are stuck in the back of my upper thigh.

"No, that's not what I mean. I mean she has it all together, she is attractive and smart and knows where she is going. She's got it together and is brave. It's intimidating to have a conversation with someone who is successful and doing well."

I'm not really sure how to take this comment. It feels a little like being punished for being successful. So I stay brave, and continue. "I don't really know how to take that. I'm a nerd. It's intimidating to walk into a room with all the beautiful people and talk to them when you feel like you don't belong. It's really, really hard."

"But you seem so confident. Don't you, like, talk in front of people for work and stuff?"

"Yeah, that's different, though. I'm so nervous in social situations. I just totally dork out."

"Well, I think you are pretty inspiring, so please take it the right way."

As the session wraps up, I leave confused, once again, and a little saddened about being compared to Amanda from *Melrose Place*. Do I really come across as a hard-arse? Have I practiced being so strong, so cool on the exterior that any softness has disappeared? Was the comparison supposed to be a compliment or an insult?

I try to look at the intent and come to realise something that perhaps I haven't realised before. Anyone can feel vulnerable or intimidated and make assumptions. I certainly have. I have assumed that the beautiful rockstar group of friends I have somehow collected are all confident and could never feel intimidated because, hey, they are beautiful, they are smart, they are kind and gorgeous. They are also as human as the rest of us. I'm learning a lesson in judgement, and realising that just because we see something desirable in others does not mean they don't see something desirable in us.

I'm not saying that narcissists don't exist, on either side of brains or beauty. Intellectual snobs who think they are somehow better than others who have learned different skills outside of classrooms and university halls. Genetically blessed beauties who have no problem in thinking they are better than someone who has turned to food as a source of emotional problem-solving, without understanding any of the backstory of the person who has been through it.

I like that Bakes has made me think differently. I like that my own thinking has been pushed, my own assumptions challenged, in a nice way. Never in a million years would I have seen myself in that way. Possibly because I find it a lot easier to see the good in others, and the flaws in me.

I find it easier to be kind to others than to be kind to me. I find it easier to think others are worthy of all the great things in life than to think I might be worthy of great things, too.

He's a very easy person to like. Pity I'm still a chickenshit. This whole 'being vulnerable' thing is harder than I thought. Have I spent so much time, effort and energy in my life being strong, toughening up, taking on the universe and God in whatever shit they could throw at me that I have completely fucked up the story of what it means to be brave? I hands-down do not question my resilience. I do not question my love of life or adventure. I do not question my love of helping others and being generous – sometimes to the point of sacrifice. I do question my ability to feel fully. To really be awkward in the sense of being vulnerable.

I think back through my list, and how I am being brave, and what questions I have avoided finding out the answer to. Crush or no crush, I don't think Bakes realises he is actually a catalyst to my own bravery.

There is one big thing on the list. One that has a time limit on it. One that if this person dies, I will live out the rest of my life wondering, *What if?*. One question that involves my mum, and whether my lack of bravery and my struggle to find my voice such a long time ago actually caused a butterfly effect on her life and the decisions she made.

This next act of bravery, this next awkward conversation, will have to wait until the return from Vegas. This one takes planning and thought. I'm glad I've got the trip to think on it and plan it out. I have given it thought for so many years. It is one of those secrets that my dad died not knowing about. My older sister knew. It has bugged me for years. But first, Vegas. Breathe, Belle, breathe. Just breathe.

6

JUNE

*B*reathe, Belle, breathe. Look at where you are. You are on the edge of this amazing, glorious world. Can you believe it? You are here. Really here. Adventure Belle lives on! Yasss!

I look down at my black runners, dangling over the edge of the cliff. I have found my rock. My rock that juts out into the void. Strong and steadfast. Shaped slowly over millions of years, this rock would have been made by small, subtle changes. It's part of a bigger picture, this ledge, where I can look back to the edge and see Lauren and Sam. They look like, well, not ants, but teeny, tiny collectable figurines about the size of my pinky finger.

"It's awesome, guys! Want to come out?" I call out across the abyss.

I had found a way to climb down and out, past two other tourists, before dropping to my knees to crawling right out to the ledge so I could dangle my legs into the mouth of Mother Earth. If I slip, I'll be smaller than a Tic Tac being swallowed whole.

Lauren and Sam call out, "Nah, we're all good! You can have that."

Breathe, Belle. Breathe. Grand. Grandiose. Some experiences really don't have words that can describe the feeling. Stillness. The stillness of sitting on this rock and looking out at one of the most amazing views ever.

I've made it. The perfect thinking spot. I could stay here forever and become part of the rock. There is nothing I have ever seen quite like it. It's the dimensions that I just can't fathom.

When you stand on the beach and look out at the ocean, where all you can see is a horizon of blue-green water with no real fathomable end in sight, you don't always appreciate the fact that that big, vast body, despite all its movement, looks relatively flat.

When you sit on a rock just over 6000 feet above the bottom of an earthly abyss, looking out to see a horizon of red, yellow, purple and brown earth with no real fathomable end in sight, it is full of movement, despite all of the Grand Canyon's stillness. The highs, lows, curves, bends, changes in colour and light, and depths of the earth leave my friend the green lady looking rather plain as she reaches towards the shore.

I think of the power of the ocean in calming my mind that day in summer, and now, here I am with the power of the earth. One klutzy move and I'll end up on the news networks back home as the idiot who tripped and fell to her death.

So while I contemplate life and death, sitting out on this rock, I try to think about whether I am being brave enough with my life. Where the lines are between being brave and being stupid. More so, where are the lines between being vulnerable and protecting my own self-worth? I can be an over-giver and leave myself open to hurt. So how do I hold that balance between the hardness of the earth and the softness of the ocean?

I don't really have the answer, but I do know, from sitting on this rock, that I want to live a life full of experiences. Big, small, happy, sad. I can't be closed off anymore. I need to be brave. Not resilient – I have that shit in the bag. I need to be brave. With owning my worth, and with opening my heart.

Lauren calls out to me if I am coming back from the edge, so I turn around, all class, and crawl back away from the edge and past the two tall American men taking selfies on selfie sticks in their utility shorts. Back to where I can estimate safely that if I do trip, I will just faceplant on more rock – I won't go over the edge to a horrible 'oh, shit, wish I had a little more grace' death.

I think of what Baker shared about how he had been to the Grand Canyon. It has been on my list for such a long time. He'd told me he had visited as a kid, and that 'grand' is probably the most appropriate word.

He was right.

I'd planned initially to hike down to the bottom, camp there, and hike out again. Sometimes I find when I tell friends what I intend on getting up to, they misinterpret the level of energy I have for going and doing stuff. I think they can misinterpret how serious I can be when I say I'm going to go and do X,Y and Z. They are all, 'Yay! We will come with you' and their energy starts out the same as mine. Give them half a day, though, and their facial expressions change to, 'What the fuck have I signed up for?'.

Anyway, the hike to the bottom didn't happen. Climbing out to sit on a rock and just think about life. That happened. Planning the conversation with Hamish. That still had to happen.

We are nearing the end of our time in the States, and yet we still have a few more items on the list to go, even though we have ticked off a few here. We missed a couple, too. Sometimes, you are just going to be a chicken, and if it is not going to change your life dramatically, if you don't really want to know the answer, that is okay.

As midday approaches, Lauren and Sam leave me to hike back on my own while they catch the bus back to El Tovar, our meeting spot. I estimate that I'll be back there by 6 pm to meet them for wine.

This space to just walk and think allows me to think of everything we have done since landing in the States. Talk about the trip of a lifetime. A mumventure.

Lauren and I had left our roles as mothers, wives (well, Lauren, not me) and business chicks behind to fly from Perth to Brisbane and then on to Los Angeles, where we had Thelma and Louise'd it to Vegas for the business mastermind before a stint at the Grand Canyon and a stop at the Bellagio.

We had driven down Rodeo Drive and cranked a bit of AC/DC in our convertible Mustang. Worked out how to drive on the other side of the road with the help of using 'righty tighty, lefty loosey' to turn corners and not end up on the wrong side of the road.

When Lauren and I decided to come to Vegas, we talked to great extent about things we would do. Stay in Santa Monica. Go to Muscle Beach. Try to find Keanu Reeves and see if he would go on a date with me. Eat Mexican food – my first food love. Maybe go on a date with Keanu Reeves and eat Mexican food.

The closest I came to eating Mexican food with Keanu was buying a burrito from a street taco van where the dude failed to give me my change from my 10 dollar bill – it was a six-dollar vegie burrito and it was delicious.

Once we had our Mexican feast, we sat on a park bench, enjoying yet another round of Mexican amazingness that LA had to offer.

I love going to new places. It doesn't matter whether it is a track in a state forest, a new stretch of beach near where I live, or a café with a worn old leather couch that I can sit and watch people from. I like eating the food, watching the people, observing the culture, smelling the air.

The air along Santa Monica Boulevard where we sat with our street burritos had a weird smell. If it were to be bottled as a perfume, I'd describe it as follows:

The free-love-style scent begins with fresh notes of salty sea air, punctuated with earthy undertones of communal spliff-sharing haze, followed by surprising and unexpected bursts of dog shit. Sure to capture your attention.

Smells and all, I loved Santa Monica. The palm trees, the sand that stretches for what seemed like miles to the water's edge, the seals that could be spotted on the pier with an 'Oh, hey humans, whatcha doin'?'-type attitude. They look like if they were packing cash, they might just buy you a beer and talk about the state of politics.

The big shock, though, given that this is a first-world nation, was the number of homeless. It's not like there aren't homeless people in Australia. Even where I live in suburbia, there is a homeless issue. I often wonder what happened in people's lives to lead them to here. Whether they have experienced trauma or made some life choices that took them down the road to homelessness.

While Lauren and I were sitting on the bench with our food, I noticed one guy. He was tall, wearing dark blue jeans that looked dirty and a dark blue jumper, beanie on, brown hair poking out underneath. He could have been an unwashed Keanu, yet his facial features said otherwise. He had been wandering the bins, looking for food. Eventually, homeless Keanu made his way over towards our bench and the bin nearby.

I didn't particularly need to eat all my burrito. It was huge. Enough to feed two mes, if I'm being fair. Plus the, um, 'internal freeway' was getting a bit of a traffic jam – actually, a food baby was in the making, if you get my drift. So the more burrito I sent into the mix, the worse.

He hovered just near the bench where we were sitting. Quietly. I looked at my burrito. I looked at homeless Keanu. I whispered to Lauren.

"Hey, Lauren… I'm going to give the rest of my burrito to homeless Keanu. I can't eat it all, and if I put it in the bin, he's clearly going to eat it, anyway. I think it would be a pretty shitty thing to do in front of someone who is clearly hungry."

So… I asked homeless Keanu if he would like my half a burrito.

He was polite and gracious, accepting my half-eaten burrito. Probably had better manners than my kids. Definitely appreciated food more than my kids do. Turned out homeless Keanu's name was Dan. I didn't really know how to have a conversation with homeless Keanu/Dan. I'm not even sure if there is an etiquette – whether you make someone feel more or less human by extending a connection. All conversations I would like to learn to navigate on a different day.

My biases and flaws did get the better of me. I am a flawed human. Thoughts started seeping in. My brain and its fears and biases ticked over.

I wonder if Dan has head lice?

I wonder when the last time was that he had a shower?

I wonder when was the last time someone hugged him?

Instead of asking him if he would like to sit with us and having a conversation with him, I started visualising getting lice on my last day in Santa Monica, knowing full well that shortly afterwards, Lauren and I would be on the road to Vegas. I didn't particularly want to turn up at the mastermind with head lice.

Awkwardly, I said to Dan that we had to go, and wished him well.

He thanked us for the burrito once more, as we scurried away like scaredy cats back to the safety of the Palihouse before deciding we should go do a little bit of shopping before hitting the road the next day.

I wish I'd been braver, hugged Dan and said that it was nice to meet him. But I didn't. I need to work on being a better person.

As we wandered the stores at 9 pm, I leaned in and told Lauren that I was having some Jorge issues. Jorge was my newly named food baby. Not in the sense that he is a chef and brings me food – in my dreams. More in the sense that I have a terrible, somewhat un-PC habit of naming any food babies after the nationality of the food.

I really should have a rule – actually, I do have a rule, 'If it's made of wheat or made of meat, then it's something I really should not eat!' I got diagnosed with Crohn's disease in my early twenties and it took me time to learn my trigger foods. I sometimes choose to ignore it, though, to the detriment of my digestion, creating a family of food babies that get named along the way.

Naming food babies started as a joke when I attended an entrepreneur program with a lady and her husband who I'd met about three years prior. She was an older lady; let's call her Sonya. It was the middle of summer, and I was wearing a dress.

Anyway, I'd been eating a lot of chocolate croissants for breakfast. My French baby was on point. I'd predict that I was at around four-months-along level of food baby, going by my side profile. I actually didn't think I looked that bad – I probably should have sent Jo a pic of my outfit and she would have pointed out the error of my ways.

As I arrived, feeling okay about myself, Sonya made a beeline for me. Not just any old beeline. A beeline that older ladies make when think they have sniffed out a pregnancy bump to rub. I don't know when society decided it was okay to go up and rub a questionable bump, but hey, it happened. I saw Sonya approaching, thinking, *Wow, she remembered me from last time we met, and she is going to give me a hug.* As she approached, her hand went straight in and rested on my food baby. Her eyes widened as her maternal experience started to shine.

Sonya was smaller than me in stature, so she looked up with her blue-grey eyes and beautiful silver bob, a smile starting to beam on her face.

"Oh, how wonderful – when are you due?"

I was quite amused by the whole thing, and instantly prepared myself for the awkwardness that was about to come across Sonya's beautiful, ageing face.

"Oh, any day now, Sonya. I'm calling him Jacques."

Sonya looked perplexed. The bump is not big enough to be due any day. "I'm sorry?"

I smiled and broke the tension with a chuckle.

"Sorry, gorg. It's a French food baby, not human. There will be no pitter-patter of little feet – the baby-making shop closed down about four years ago!"

Her jaw dropped with embarrassment. I laughed again. It was not the first time I had to deal with comments on my body, and it probably wouldn't be the last. Unless, of course, I go back to being vegan and stop eating wheat. Then the comments might be, 'Hey, you are in pretty good nick for your age.' Damn straight!

I hugged Sonya, and told her not to worry about it, and told her the story of a Thai flight attendant who let me cut the queue to board a plane because she thought I was pregnant with my third child.

Naming food babies became my totally politically incorrect way of talking about digestion challenges without saying, 'Yeah, nah, I'm not preggers, I just haven't *been* in like five days because I've been chowing down on processed foods, but thanks for making the assumption that because I am female, and look like I am still within childbearing years, that I therefore must be pregnant.' Go equality.

So, with that in mind, I considered the fact that Jorge may even have a twin sister. As I started to talk to Lauren – who was way more aware of how un-PC I was sounding right now – about Jorge, she suggested ever so kindly that perhaps we should leave the conversation about my food babies until later.

She was right. The conversation didn't happen until the mastermind days later, when Jorge was stuck.

I stop along the Grand Canyon and watch two little American girls ride by on bikes with their mum.

"Hey Mom! There's that lady – she is walking faster than we are riding! Can we be quick at this stop please?"

The mum replies, "It doesn't matter, girls, let's just enjoy the view. You are doing great."

"Mommy! I need the pottie!" the youngest one calls out.

"Well, we might have to go off the trail, sweetheart, there isn't a bathroom here."

I chuckle as I stop at a point called The Abyss, thinking about my embarrassing bathroom situation from the mastermind.

―――――

What are you trying to be, Jorge? The star of the year?

Shit! There I was standing in the bathroom of the Vegas McMansion. Marble floors. Beautiful lighting. Teak cupboards. Brass taps. About to be ruined. What a predicament. I mean, really! Year of Awkward?

My Mexican love affair had left me food baby pregnant, stranded in a foreign country with a group of strangers, and alone.

I stared, horrified. How could this be happening? I mean, I was just talking about the fact that I needed more content. So, thanks, universe, God, whatever. I appreciate you. Thanks for delivering this 'gift' of embarrassment and a lesson in asking for help so swiftly.

I pressed the button again.

Nothing.

Well, nothing but more water in the bowl.

It was not a toilet like the ones back in Australia. Australian toilets suck the contents down, and then refill the bowl. American toilets – well, this American toilet – filled up the bowl first. This toilet was evil. It was an evil – going-to-embarrass-the-shit-out-of-you, literally – toilet designed to humiliate and scar anyone who has just delivered a burrito baby into the world.

I pressed the button for the third time, risking my life, praying that the evidence would disappear. The water level was almost at the top – there was NOTHING I could do.

I knew that if I were to attempt one more watery send-off with Jorge, a flood would be imminent. A flood where Jorge would be all over the decadent second-floor bathroom in the Vegas McMansion.

I started freaking out.

Shit, shit, shit, shit, shit, shit, shit. I opened cupboards, looking for A N Y T H I N G that I could use to unblock Jorge.

The best I could find was a scrappy-looking piece of wire. It was a bit thicker than a coat hanger. I bent over the toilet bowl and poked at Jorge, trying to force him down. Nothing.

Why? Why is it always the Aussie chick at the international mastermind thing who manages to block the toilet? Why?

I needed to try to muster the courage to call for help. Someone who could come and maybe do something. This was going to be sooo embarrassing. But at least Lauren knew Jorge.

"Lauren! Lauren!" I whisper-screamed out the bathroom door and down the staircase, hoping she could hear me. "Lauren! I need your help! We have a situation!"

"What do you mean, we?"

"Well, I don't know what to do – I need your help."

"So *you* have a situation?"

"Yes! I have a situation! I'm freaking out! And it's totally awkward and I need your help!"

"What happened?"

"Well, I accidentally asked the universe for something else to be brave with, and now this has happened. It's Jorge! He's stuck! Like, really stuck."

I looked at my gorgeous Kiwi friend with her big, blue eyes. She looked a little like a deer in headlights. I could see her thoughts: *I don't wanna be here, but here I am – in the Jorge situation, oh God.*

"Well, I can't do anything about it. What do you want me to do?"

In hushed, 'we're in the trenches together' tones, we talked about what to do. I was sure this wasn't the first time an embarrassing thing happened in Vegas. It was a first for me, though, and a first for Lauren.

"Well, what happens in Vegas… I accidentally manifested it, Lauren!"

"You certainly manifested something… ummm… extreme."

Earlier that day, I had been sitting by a pool at the McMansion house in Las Vegas chatting to Sherrie, a gorgeous, free-spirited writer, about movies, books, coaching using technology and making a living outside of the nine-to-five box.

Like me, Sherrie had taken time out from her current life to attend the women's mastermind retreat. There were 12 of us in attendance from different pockets of the globe. Me, the token Aussie; Lauren, from NZ – who I'd talked into coming with me even though she didn't feel ready; Americans from different parts of the US – including our hosts Sam and

Kathy; a couple of Canadians who could belt out any song on a Disney playlist; and the Spain-based Brit, Sian.

Sherrie was from Newfoundland in Canada, had a German home base and was currently sailing with her husband and two small kids on a boat around Saint Martinique and other wanderlust destinations. To say I found her fascinating would be an understatement. She was living proof that you can have any life you wish if you are brave, if you make a plan and if you take action.

As this mastermind event would have it, when there is sunshine, downtime and a pool involved, we got talking about what we did, what we were working on, and how – as two strangers – maybe we could help each other out a little.

I shared that I was up for pushing the boundary on being brave. I had committed to seeing what those pants looked like either through doing things outside my comfort zone, or being brave and finding out answers to questions I was yet to ask. I had also shared that I was okay if I looked like a loser in the process. I shared my whole 'feel the fear of falling on your face and do it anyway' philosophy.

Sherrie had designed a beautiful life. I was fascinated to learn that she supported creatives remotely, from a boat, and that her core business was coaching them to become unblocked. Helping others to be brave with their craft or business and dig deep and show their vulnerability was something we had in common. That, and sailing boats – something I had not done for years.

The talk of sailing reminded me once again of who I was. Unblocking my love of adventure during this year was about getting back to the core of who I was – not the role or responsibility, but remembering my love for life that had not been fully expressed for quite some time. It had been beached like driftwood amongst the trappings of motherhood, business and life.

Becoming unblocked was something I needed help with. So I decided to say a mantra out loud.

"Okay, universe, help me to be unblocked when it comes to being brave with love and having the big, heartfelt conversation with Hamish when I return home."

Clearly the universe got the message. Which is how Jorge ended up well and truly stuck. My intestines: unblocked. The toilet: not so much.

"Do you want me to go and get Mindy?" Lauren asks.

Mindy was also on the mastermind with us. I connected with her online, as well as Sam. As she hailed from New York with a PR background, we figured Mindy would be great to help us manage my crisis situation.

"Yes! Perfect choice. Go get her! I feel safe with Mindy! We've chatted a fair bit on Facebook before today. I can't just leave the scene with Jorge stuck in there. What would someone else think? *Yay! Look what the Aussie girl left.* It would be such poor form to leave Jorge and his mess in the bathroom. This is freaking embarrassing! I felt like this should be in a movie."

"Well, if it were going to happen to anyone, Belle, it would be you…"

"Well, can you help me? Please? I can't just leave!"

"Okay. I'll go find Mindy."

Mindy arrived to see me guarding the doorway like a bouncer who needs to pee. Seeing her face, I think she had already activated PR Mode.

"What seems to be the problem – you look all flushed. Are you alright?"

"I wish I was all flushed – that's, ah, actually the problem."

"Belle, you really do have a way with words," Lauren said.

"Thanks. I just wish right now I had a way with plumbing systems. Your toilets are weird! We don't have these in Australia."

"Okay, well, how bad is the situation?"

"Pretty bad. Hey, remember the plunger we used to whack the piñata on the first night?"

"Yeah, sure – it's pretty big and brand new."

"Well, both those things are good. Can you find it?"

"I'm on it."

She disappeared for about five minutes, returning with the plunger and a lesson. A lesson that will probably stick with me forever.

Sometimes, you will literally find yourself in the shit. And you will need to ask for help. No matter how embarrassed or dumb or stupid you feel. Sometimes you just won't be equipped with the tools, knowledge or skills to solve a problem you have created, like Jorge. While you could do the best with what you have, like a piece of wire, the best option can be to do the best with what other people have. As long as you ask for their help.

I ended up gaining new skills on the mastermind: plumbing skills. I'd never had to plunge a toilet – but then, I'd never blocked a toilet with a food baby either. I also vowed to give up meat and wheat and maybe lay off the creation of food babies for a while. Accidental vegan, here I come!

I continue the hike back to our meeting point, to be greeted by my two friends and what I can only describe as the best nachos I have ever eaten in my life.

We sit and watch the sunset over the canyon. It brings a tear to my eye. This world is truly full of beauty. I feel like that adventurous soul I had lost has found her way back. It's a new moon, and over our nachos and wine, to celebrate life, we talk about doing a new moon ceremony around the campfire when we get back to our tent.

While the Jorge situation was tricky to navigate, my vulnerability faces another challenge that night in the canyon. The goal of the ceremony? Write down and burn anything that no longer serves us, and welcome in good intentions. We each choose to show gratitude to one another and say some beautiful, positive things.

I don't realise that each of us is to read out what we are releasing and what we want to let in. I sit by the fire, and think about what to write. I feel like I have done a fair amount of work on being brave to this point. I know I still have a way to go. The conversation with Hamish that has to happen. My questions about my crush on Baker and if I am imagining things. The desire to write, and be fully free to express who I am without fear.

My paper simply says: *I release feelings of worthlessness and welcome in being vulnerable so I can be worthy of great love from myself and from others.*

Upon my turn to read out loud, I burst into tears.

A lifetime of tears. Abandonment tears. Shame tears. Judgement tears. Rejection tears. Regret tears.

Tears which had been dammed up to create my exterior strength, resilience and a laugh-my-way-through-shit type of attitude. In this lifetime, I had crafted a way to bury vulnerabilities deep down. It's not easy admitting that I switched off parts of myself. The 'I can get hurt' parts. Self-preservation, I guess. I don't want to be so strong anymore that I didn't know how to be soft. How to feel. I want to be open enough to joy to accept any pain that might come with it if things don't work out.

So here I am, in the middle of a joy-filled adventure with women who are my safe space in which to be vulnerable – a circle that is a test for whether I can actually be brave. They test my own inner truth.

Staring at the fire, the realisation I still have internal work to do with heart-based bravery washes over me. Yes, I can confront big situations, like death, asking for money, chats with my kids. I'm just a human who still has a way to go in letting the light of life crack all the way back in.

If I want to go after true happiness, whatever that looks like, I have to prepare for feeling true hurt again. They cohabitate. I don't want to crack the door to a life that I want, just enough to see what is out there, and not be brave enough to step through it. I don't want my belief in what I think I deserve to hold me back. I want to believe big.

I want to open that door a little wider, no matter how weird and uncomfortable. I am going all-in for the step through and step forward, even if I am unsure of my footing. I have fallen down plenty of times, so I know how to get back up. The Grand Canyon has helped me remember that. Plus, even if I'm not sure of how to get back up, I know I can ask for help. I mean, I really do have the most amazing gang of girlfriends to help me figure it out.

Listening to the others, the vulnerability wells over into the night. Tears flow. Bare feet press into the ground, and one by one – at least for this fleeting moment – we are all connected. Not by business masterminding, or goals, or strategies, but by the freedom to just *be*.

With a deep breath, I focus on holding space to be kind to myself. I commit to welcoming in bravery and start to think of the next point on my list when I return home. I think of the story of the little girl who has been wondering if her misinterpretation of bravery was the reason for a move that has haunted her for the better part of 35 years.

When I was 10, our family ceremoniously packed up and relocated to the arse end of the world. Not quite Antarctica, but close enough.

Before we left, another fourth-grader got a Cabbage Patch Kid. I wanted one, too. I wanted to go through the adoption process. I wanted to show my commitment to a stuffed doll – a stuffed doll that, seven years later, ended up playing the role of Mitch Buchannon alongside Disco Barbie as CJ in homemade movie parodies of *Baywatch*, where he ended up in the pool and died a sad, stuffed-toy-decaying death.

I had been nagging for a Cabbage Patch Kid constantly. Not the fake one named Angela that my dad had got me from the markets as a sign of trying to please me. I was ungrateful, not really understanding how much money the real ones were. I wanted the real deal. Not Angela, who was taller than the 'real' cabbage patch dolls. Not Angela, who was missing the Xavier Roberts signature on her butt cheek.

I nagged my mum, my dad, my stepdad, whichever parental figure was present. Every. Single. Day. Past my December birthday – where no Cabbage Patch Kid turned up. Over the long stretch of the Nullarbor Plain. Onto the ship that took us to our new destination.

Our new destination was a little bit of a shock to me. No friends. Two TV channels to choose from; only one with cartoons on a Saturday. The worst at this point? The toilet was outside. And it didn't flush. We moved from modern suburban conveniences to an old – like, built-by-the-first-settlers old – farmhouse on a tiny island where the grass was thin, the summer sun was scarce and the sheep were aplenty.

Our Christmas tree was the saddest little branch stuck in dirt with one piece of tinsel strung around it. It was supposed to be a big tree, but man, this thing was sad. You couldn't decorate this twig as it'd just collapse under the weight of the tinsel. So it sat in the corner, surrounded by a couple of presents, and I remember thinking for the first time that this move – this apparent 'adventure' – sucked.

We had goats. We had chickens. What happened to having a dog like other people? I saw my mum make cheese from goats' milk. I watched chickens' heads get chopped off, staring in disbelief that the chicken was still squawking while its body ran around headless, chasing the executioner. There is some stuff that you can't unsee. Some memories just get seared into your brain. I don't even know what the memory selection process is in terms of determining which ones will make you, shake you, or break you, and which ones just get deleted as being of no use. Maybe the ones we don't keep are unable to shape us or add any real value in creating us.

Anyway, the chicken, which became Christmas lunch, is one that is seared into my head. Freaky.

I was not really part of the 'Hey, let's move to a remote island and live on a farm with no inside toilet' team. I missed my friends. I missed the beach. I missed my real dad. I had no idea why we had just upped and moved.

Christmas day rolled around and I opened my present. Lo and behold, I got a 'We are sorry we have just ripped you away from your life and stuck you on a farm so hopefully this makes up for it' Cabbage Patch Kid. Yay! His name was Kim. He wore a blue-and-red soccer outfit, had tiny Adidas-style shoes, socks, the all-important Xavier Roberts signature on his butt, and curly auburn hair. I was over the moon.

You had the option to change their names. My sister got a doll named Kate, which she decided to instead name after our big sister, Witchy, who we knew about, but didn't really know – she never lived with us – that's a whole other story. Funnily enough, years later, our big sister had her last child before she died, whose name is Cate – spelled differently. She never knew the Cabbage Patch Kid's name. I opted to leave Kim as Kim. I figured that was the name he was given, so why should it be changed?

I wanted him to keep his identity. Know his roots. Talk to him about where he came from – he was from Illinois in the US. I had received an amazing *World Atlas* from my grandfather on my dad's side for my birthday before we left. I looked up Illinois in the US, and learned that there was a lot of farmland there. I figured Kim would probably like living here with the outside toilet, headless chickens and the 20-gazillion sheep.

We rolled through the Christmas break and it came time to enrol in school. The school where I would one day be mercilessly teased for the jumper I wore. The jumper that had belonged to a wealthy kid only a week before and was donated to the op-shop where my mum went. The kid who found it important to point out that the new kid was wearing their discarded clothes. That kid was an arsehat.

Except my name was no longer the same. My name had been changed – my surname, that is. And I didn't really understand why.

I was no longer Belle Lockerby. I was Belle Someone-else.

I questioned my mum as to why my name was no longer Lockerby. Her reply was that it was easier to do this as a family unit.

It never sat right with me.

It also never sat right with me that I didn't get to see my dad for two years. I just didn't understand the move, but I did wonder if I had something to do with it.

No matter how much my biological parents hated each other – and they did hate each other – they inadvertently shaped what I thought a successful family unit should look like. They shaped what I thought co-parenting should look like. They shaped what I thought failure, sacrifice and generosity should look like.

Cutting one parent off from the other out of spite was not what I thought it would look like.

It is this move, this changing of the name, this being cut off from my dad, that has bugged me for years. More than the shitful kid who tormented me for wearing their jumper. It has bugged me because I think my lack of bravery in saying something may have contributed to it.

I have carried secrets for years, and some of them I will continue to carry, as to let them out into the light will not do any good to anyone. Not me, not the surviving members of my family – no one.

But this move, this reason for moving to the arse end of the world, bugs me. It bugs me because I wonder if somehow I became the catalyst for my mum's later depression. If I may have made her feel like she failed, because I was too scared to tell the truth.

I've toyed for years with whether I should try to find out why we moved. Why my name was changed. I only have one person left that I can ask about it, and for me, that would be my next act of bravery. The next, really difficult, conversation to have.

I guess I am looking to find out about this move for a number of reasons. Firstly, I have one parental-type figure left in my life. If he were to die, I know I would regret never asking the question. But I have wondered if having this go unanswered in my life could be something that I am happy with.

Secondly, I want to know if I contributed to the move. To her depression. Ultimately, to her death. I am not particularly worried about the response, or the outcome. I am no longer tied to events. At least, that is what I tell myself. I am driven by curiosity. I'm not on a witch hunt – of others, or of myself. I just want to understand why. Did my definition of bravery at 10 years of age create a chain of events? I want to know if there was any knowledge around the abuse. This is something that I do not want to live out the rest of my life with a big-arse question mark over. I need to at least try to understand the why. Then I can put it to bed.

I decide that I need to tackle the big conversation with my stepdad, Hamish, when I get home.

7

JULY

*I*t's Thursday. I've just done my super-quick surf before the ballet run to the city. Even with conditions a little on the choppy side, I'm loving the surf in winter – the water feels warmer than the winter air. The beach is fairly quiet. As I stand under the beach shower, evidence of being wiped out and standing back up again shows. I may have exfoliated my ears, with the amount of sand I'm picking out. Water has gathered around the inside of my wetsuit calves, giving me surfer cankles. Some excess weight has dropped since returning home from Vegas, in more ways than one. I bend down, squeezing the water out, thinking on the stretches Baker has given me.

I'm sure there are trigger points in my back and my legs from acupuncture that have given me a backbone to be brave. I turn off the shower taps outside the surf club, feeling the breeze kick up. Fresher than a freezer with a mint spray. Brrr. Physically, I'm so ready to race home for a hot shower. Mentally, I'm prepping for calling Hamish. I'm future-forecasting how the conversation might go. I'm getting ready to find out what I'm actually made of.

Stripping off the wetsuit, I feel like I might also be stripping off my emotional superhero cape. I mean, it's heavy. Weighted with high expectations I've placed on myself. Mentally, I'm giving myself permission to have the courage to be awkward, vulnerable and feel again. I pack my trusty giant yellow board in the back of the car and head home for the next shower. A hot one.

I reflect on how this all got started. This whole 'Year of Bravery' thing, instigated by my mid-summer ocean meltdown.

I can remember a moment I stood in a room with all my business mums and looked a talented, young photographer named Amanda in the eye. She'd asked me how she could be herself and share her story, and did she have to be super-professional like in her previous corporate life? I'd responded, saying, "There is great strength in choosing vulnerability."

Because I know that struggle to be who we really want to be – leftovers from 'fit in the box' corporate conditioning. I remember thinking, *Geez, Belle, you are full of shit. You are great at bravery in business, but not all areas of life.*

I've come pretty far this year so far and been brave in lots of ways, but to live my truth, I need to step up my game.

I'm still worried I might die with a business brain that's been liberated and a heart that's all locked up. That my only acts of bravery will be the physical or financial ones. Learn to surf, run marathons, white-water raft. Start a business. Negotiate my financial value with men in blue suits, to be paid more in one day than I earned in three weeks. Hike mountains. Hoo-fucking-ray. No acts of spiritual or emotional bravery in sight. What life lessons will I teach my kids?

I don't want to be made of stone. I'm at a real risk of shutting my heart and feelings and emotions off if I can't start being massively brave, and if I can't do it in my 'Year of Bravery', when will I? How am I even going to approach the weight of this conversation?

I know I'm resilient. I know purely from the fact that after all sorts of shit, I'm still standing. Still smiling, and still looking for the best in people and in life. But this wall around my heart has got to go. It's time to do some major renovations and smash a couple of walls. Starting with this big-arse motherfucker that had served me well for a long time.

Hamish, my stepdad, has created a brand-new life. The person I knew as a child is very different to the person I know as an adult. Except he is the only one I can ask this question. I don't even know if he would be up for a conversation, with his new life and all.

I play the scenarios through. He could say, "No, I'm not up for the conversation." If that is the case, that will be the end of it. I'll be okay with it being unanswered, but at least I will have tried. He could say, "Yes, I'm up for the conversation." Then, I'll have to think about how I can handle it with calm, grace and no attachment to the outcome.

Then there are the potential answers. I'll have to deal with those.

With a big breath, I pick up my phone and call Hamish. "Hey, Hamish. I'm wondering if you are free for a chat? It's an in-person chat, and it's not going to be an easy chat for me. I have questions to do with Mum."

"I'm home now – the family are here, is that okay?"

"Well, I will need to talk to you in private, so please check with them if they are okay with that. If not, it's fine."

"That's okay, we can sit outside. I actually live behind your dad's old house now."

"Oh. Well that's just a bit weird. He'd probably hate that."

"Not to worry, come on over."

"I'll see you in about 20 minutes."

I hop in my car and start to go over how the conversation is going to go. I work to calm myself and breathe as I drive. As a coping mechanism, that poker game face from business negotiations comes back into play; I can use those skills to navigate my way through what is going to be a really awkward and tricky conversation.

I just don't want to live in the dark on matters that I'd like answers to. I want to know what being free of the 'what if's feels like. I've figured out I can surf – no matter how much I feel like a complete dork as the only mum in a sea of dads. I've figured out I can have awkward conversations with my kids on sex, erections, potentially getting out there and dating again, and watching their little faces either go "yay" or "ew gross, why are you telling me this?"

The magnitude of this conversation starts to sink in. This is a big one.

As I arrive, it seems weird to pretty much be at the back of my childhood house where I learned to climb trees, test out theories on quicksand, and be a scared little girl hiding in the toilet from giant – okay, tiny – frogs.

The scared little girl steps with me into the breeze, our hair whirling around. I'm trying to show her, and me, how to be brave. I whisper to her that the breeze is one of change. That it's time to speak up. No more hiding. That vulnerability is a good thing. That no matter what, we will be okay. That our happiness, our truth, our peace, counts. That it is better to be brave and do the scary thing over sitting in the comfortable, growth-stunting safety of unhappiness and familiarity.

I pull my car into the driveway, starting to fidget with the yellow, blue and pink beads on my crystal bracelets with my left hand, before switching to twisting the rose-gold and silver wave rings around on my thumb with my right hand. It's how I channel my nervous energy. A long time ago, as a teenager, when I'd talk to Hamish I used to zip my little silver cross on my neck back and forth. Some habits you don't quite grow out of.

I knock on the door, rehearsing my opening conversation, reminding myself that the answers I receive don't matter – the action of having the conversation does. The process matters, the kindness matters, the truth matters, not the outcome.

"Hey, Hamish. Nice to see you! Thanks for doing this."

I haven't seen Hamish since Christmas. We may see each other once a year, if that. I could probably count the number of times on my hands that I have seen him since my mum died. Not out of dislike, just out of distance.

"Hi, Bee! Come in. The family are inside."

I say hello to them all and thank them for allowing me to steal Hamish away for a conversation. I'm sure it must be weird having me there. I'm not blood. I'm a living ghost from his past. Yet his family, in all our interactions, have only ever treated me with acceptance and kindness. How human beings should treat each other.

The feelings of trepidation are high. Internally, I work to calm myself and remember that I am not attached to the outcome. That my intention is simply to understand if there is any information. That the contents, whatever they are, of the information don't matter. What matters is being brave. Stepping into this abyss and seeing where my feet land. Opening and closing doors simultaneously. Moving forward with whatever happens.

"Can we get you tea or coffee?"

I'm sure he looks nervous, too. This man who I was probably – no, not probably, who I *was* – a shit of a kid towards at certain points. The man who, at times during my childhood, was one that I earmarked as my greatest foe. The man I learnt to do battle with – mentally and verbally at times. The man I stood up to, who inadvertently sparked the fiery fierceness inside that would see me fight for myself – not just as a child, but as an adult – with the big powers that be. Bring it the fuck on, God, universe, whatever. Until I realised that asking for battles was tiring and draining. And maybe I should be asking for great love, happiness and peace.

Today was not a battle, though. Today was a peace talk.

"Tea would be great, thanks. Um, can we sit somewhere outside?"

"Sure. Follow me."

"Are you sure that your family are okay with this? It's okay to say if not – I know you have a whole new life, and they are very good, but I still understand that this may be weird for them, so I appreciate the chance to chat."

"No, it's not a problem. They all know that I had a life before. And if it ever was an issue, they would speak up and talk about things. So... I'll just get you some tea, and then we can have a chat, okay?"

As I sit out the back on the garden chair, I can see my old backyard. The one where the frogs inhabited the swimming pool. The large tree I climbed. Once again, I whisper to the little girl to be brave, that no matter what, things will be carried away on the breeze, and it will be okay.

He returns with the tea. The verbal Band-Aid is now obvious. We both know something is about to be ripped. Him, not sure of the topic. Me, not sure of the response. So I start.

"This is not going to be an easy conversation. But you are one of the last people from a time and place that is still around, and who can maybe help me understand what happened."

Hamish pauses. I can see him considering how to handle this. "Is it to do with your mother?"

"Sort of – yes."

"Okay," he accepts, "well, you need to be prepared that you may not like the answers. Are you okay with that?"

I consider this, wondering if he thinks that maybe it is about the affair he had with my mum, if he even realises that I know about it. Which I did. I knew a hell of a lot thanks to her breakdowns that I was perhaps not equipped to handle. I knew a hell of a lot thanks to my dad and his afternoon truth serum sessions on a second-coming Saturday.

I had been the negotiation pawn in their games to inflict hurt on each other. Apparently, aged 12 and beyond, you are fully equipped to handle all sorts of adult shit you have no idea about. Yet, they also, like Hamish, taught me to fight for me, when I sat them both down at 13 – separately, of course, as some peace talks can't happen in the same room – and told them that I loved them both, and that enough was enough. The he said/she said/did had to stop.

It didn't stop fully, but it did reduce them to their own adult shit instead of them igniting emotional warfare bombs about each other and asking me to hold them while they blew up in my heart.

"Yes, Hamish. I'm okay with whatever answers you give. I need you to know, though, that this is not a witch hunt. I'm not defined by anything that I am about to ask you. I don't feel any anger, hate, or like a victim at all. I let all that go a long, long time ago. I am purely just seeking to understand something."

"Okay, well, shoot. Let's do this, hey?"

I take a deep breath. I stare at the tea and think about how to dive into what is a really hard conversation. I try to find the words.

"I'm trying to understand about the move to the butt crack of the world. I'm trying to understand why my name was changed, and I'm hoping you can shed some light on this. I know my mum hated my dad, and I'm wondering if there was anything that she said about doing this."

"Well, you are right. She hated your father with a passion. She thought that maybe he had, uh, done the wrong thing by you, if you get what I mean."

"You mean abuse?"

"Yes."

"My dad never laid a hand on me, and it has bugged me for years that perhaps she made this assumption because I was too scared to speak up about what actually happened."

"So something did happen?"

"Yes. At best, I would describe it as severe sexual bullying. At its worst, I would describe it as child abuse. And it happened right under her nose while she visited friends. Is this what you thought I was going to ask you about?"

"No, not quite. I'm so sorry that happened to you."

"Don't be. It started when I was six and occurred on and off over the years until I was 11. Did you have any inkling that something may have happened?"

"I'm worried that this happened on my watch. I had collected you for your mother one day when you were eight or nine. I thought I'd help out and unpacked your clothes to do the laundry, and found blood on your underwear."

"Oh," I say. I'm surprised, and not surprised at the same time, as I had been questioned. I had answered falsely. I had answered falsely, as when you are held inside a brown cupboard as a child with a pocketknife against your cheek and threats of your family being hurt if you dare say a word, you pretty much don't dare say a word. You are frozen with fear while your tiny hands are placed where they should not be placed. A sick game. One where physical size and intimidation paralyses a little girl who was previously brave. A little girl who decides proving survival, working hard and getting the fuck out of her neighbourhood to never return is a good life plan.

My mum sat down the hallway drinking English breakfast tea with her friend while this happened. I was eight.

A memory floods back in of being ashamed of my body in the bath. Of not wanting my mum, or anyone to see me. I knew exactly why I was behaving this way. I didn't know it was shame, but that is what it was. I fed it with secrecy. I was focused on protecting others around me, and I was the price. Therein was the starting pattern for putting others as more worthy than me. I was asked if something had happened. I was asked to tell the truth. I didn't.

I look up at Hamish. His eyes have welled with tears. I sit here, remaining calm. You might say cold. Maybe I am still switched off… just a bit. Maybe not. I don't know.

"I'd tried to do the right thing," he says. "I questioned you. I did all the things that adults are supposed to do to protect children from those kinds of situations. I asked, but you wouldn't budge. You were adamant that there was nothing wrong, and nothing had happened."

He paused to think of what to say next. "I don't know what else I could have done. I can only say sorry. Have you ever confronted the person about it?"

"Look, there were times as I grew up that I imagined punching him in the face, shooting him, and just sending as much hate towards him as I could muster. Then one day I just stopped. I started to wonder what kind of life he must have had to think that his actions towards me were acceptable. And then I didn't feel hate or anger, or anything. I just felt pity towards him, and eventually nothing. That someone could think treating another person – a child – so horribly was acceptable is sad in itself."

"Well, you seem like you have grown up to be well-adjusted, regardless of it."

"It's something I've had to fight for. Sometimes those fights are silent. It's hard because you make choices that you are consciously making because of those events. I never wanted to be a victim or be defined by one shitty period of my life. For me, that was handing over control of my whole, entire life to an arsehole. Why would I want to do that?"

"How do you mean, you've had to fight for it?"

"Well, sometimes it's the little things. Like being okay with the kids having a bath with their dad when they were little. It's all innocent, yet stuff still comes up – my stuff – that I have to process. As a parent, I've had to make a conscious effort to not let what happened to me change the freedom my kids have. To balance being vigilant and making sure they get an actual childhood and their innocence stays intact, with giving them the freedom to do things where my default might be to look for all the terrible things that could go wrong.

We sit in silence. I watch Hamish process what I have said and trace the edge of his teacup with his stubby finger, stopping to tap just above the handle. It's not uncomfortable silence, though. It's reflective, no, familiar. Where you can just be.

"So tell me, then, Bee, how does this relate to the move?"

"Well, I wondered if maybe, just maybe, Mum had made the assumption that my dad had done the wrong thing, and that is why she changed my surname from his name. I wonder if that contributed to the hate between them, and even if it contributed to her depression."

"I do know that she hated him, and that she mentioned she thought he did the wrong thing."

"Well, he never did. She wasn't always well, and some of the things she said were not cool."

"No, I knew your mum pretty well. And yes, it wasn't easy with her depression. You have turned into a strong, accomplished woman, though, so you should be proud of yourself."

"I am. I wouldn't be who I am without what I have been through. It's all good."

We talk more on my mum, on things that she said and did. Some things he had no awareness of. I feel like I'm clearing my dad's name of any misunderstanding. That maybe his ghost over the fence is saying 'thank you'. I feel like I have cleared him of being part of a false story that may have been the catalyst for the move.

We talk of how I ended up living in the caravan park across from the beach when I was 16, in front of the giant blue wheat silos. Another Mum decision. The same beach I returned to when she died. Where I felt forsaken, abandoned, and gave my beliefs a big middle finger.

I mean, I was a good kid. Good grades. Didn't smoke. Didn't drink. I was focused on using my brain and escaping where we lived.

I breathe in, and toy with uncovering how much Hamish knew of why I lived in a caravan park.

"Do you know why I was moved to the caravan park? Why Mum thought it was a good idea?"

"No, why?"

"Look. I know that she was not well. But her reasoning was because you and I did not get along, that you had apparently said to her one day that I needed to get a good fuck and lose my virginity, and that maybe you should do it. So she was moving me out for my own safety. I was devastated."

"Oh, Bee, I'm so sorry. I never said that."

"I wondered… Hopefully you also understand why there was such a long silence between her death and us touching base again. I know she hated my dad. I know she said she thought he had abused me. He never laid a finger on me."

My mum was troubled, not to everyone, and I know she had good points. I know she didn't have an easy life, but I certainly felt that I bore more than a child's share of things that should not have been said. Many times, I was the parent without parenting skills for her, trying to figure out the right thing to do. I had carried too many damaging secrets. I still carry some.

In this conversation, the burden of those secrets gets released.

Hamish now has insight as to the battles I have fought. Not the ones growing up with him – ours were vocal sparring matches – but the battles with my mum. They were silent and unseen, like the wars within myself for the past 20 years. Now he knows why I consciously crafted a wall of time and distance between our own connection. Just as walls can be built brick by brick, those bricks can be removed and repurposed into something more suitable.

As it nears dinnertime, Hamish's family offers me a place at the table. I explain that I have an online call to attend to, and need to get home to get lights and tech set up. Ever gracious, they pack me a takeaway container of their dinner so I don't have to worry about cooking at home.

It's in this moment that I start to realise family is not a tree – it's a forest. I thank Hamish and his family for their time, kindness and generosity, and promise to catch up again soon. Which I really should, as one day Hamish will no longer be here.

As I get back into the car, I look in the rearview mirror and catch a glimpse of the little girl who has travelled with me on this big journey. Having listened to the answers, having learned that the outcome doesn't matter, but the act of bravery does, she lets out a big sigh, putting the ghosts to rest.

Processing this conversation takes me some time. I'm kind of proud of how I handled it. I grew. I addressed something that has sat there in the land of 'what if's for as long as I can remember. But I have an answer.

Do I think that they should have pressed harder for the truth when I was a kid? No. I was resolute in what I thought was the right action at the time. Do I think that my inaction to speak up was the butterfly wing that caused a tsunami in the changing of my name? Perhaps. I'll never really know, as I never told my mum while she was alive what had actually happened.

I share this act of bravery with my closest friends. Not to look for sympathy, just to let them know that I took a leap. I am following through on being brave, in whatever form it comes in.

It's almost odd that this conversation was easier than one of the last items on my list. Telling someone I have a crush on them.

So I'm getting to the last scary heart bravery thing on my list... Dating. Shit.

And dating is going to lead to sex. Which means no clothes. Which means a man other than the father of my children, who saw my body go from what I considered its best to its worst and then land somewhere in meh-land, will see it. I want to feel good naked. I've done the work on body love before. Might be time to revisit. I know things are shifting, but not as fast as I'd like.

As I arrive home, I walk into my bathroom and look at the mirror where I often write things.

In bright pink marker pen, I write the words, "You deserve a bangin' hot bod after 40". Then things start shifting. Big time.

8

AUGUST

J'm staring at my guest presenter, listening to her beautiful English accent as she talks about SEO to my next group of entrepreneurs. We are approaching 10:30 am, and I feel my phone ping on my lap. Baker.

I let out an audible, surprised "huh!" followed by a "whoops, sorry".

Lauren is in the room with me, sitting on the opposite side – we are separated by two large tables at the front of the room and two large tables at the back.

She gives me the 'WTF was that' eyes – I read it telepathically.

I mouth to her, "Baker".

She mouths back in silence, "What? What does he want?"

In return, I give her my 'I have no fucking idea' face, shrugging my shoulders and tapping my wrist, and making a coffee hand gesture, signalling that I'll tell her at our break. I haven't seen him, or thought of him, in ages.

I stare at the text, confused.

Bakes: *Hey Belle! How are you? Thought I'd let you know I decided to overcome a fear, too. I've been diving with sharks in a cage off the coast of South Australia – and I survived (smiley face emoji).*

My phone pings again.

Bakes: *So I'm wondering if you'd like to maybe catch up for a chat.*

I stare at Lauren, pretending that I have Jedi mind powers, willing her to look my way, while she is watching the presenter. I can see her bouncing her feet up and down on the floor, channelling her own excess energy out of her body, as she is speaking to the group today, too. Her brave act.

Victoria, the presenter, calls my name. "Belle, are we right to break for 15 minutes now?"

"Oh, yeah, sure! Coffee and tea are available in the kitchen. If we can keep to time, then we will all get out of here right on 12 noon."

The group hustles out the back doors. Lauren gets up; I see her looking determined. She is wearing black canvas flats, black tights and a grey shift dress. She walks over, fast feet on the grey carpeted floor, beelining for my goofy, stupid, puzzled 'what the fuck' face.

"What's he want?"

"He wants to catch up. It's not acupuncture-related. Not advice-related. Just catching up."

"He likes you, Belle! I knew it!"

"Nooo. What do I do? Shit, shit, shit. Lauren, I'm sooo uncool. Hey, so are you all set for your speech on getting media? You'll be great!"

"Oh, no you don't! I like this topic – it's helping me not think about speaking to everyone."

"Ah, you'll nail it. Oh, look at the time. Better get to the toilet."

"Belle! Don't Jorge it!"

As I walk away, I look over my shoulder and smirk at her. "The toilet or the text?"

"Both!"

Of course, I don't know what to do with this, or what to make of this. So, as always, I call upon Jo as soon as the workshop wraps up to work out what to do.

Sitting in the vacant meeting room, I prop my phone up against a tower of little green-and-white, shoebox-size IKEA cardboard containers that I keep my workshop stationery in and FaceTime Jo.

"Hey! So, I got a text from Baker. I don't know what to do."

"What does it say?"

"Just that he's back from diving with sharks, and he wants to catch up. I think it's a joke. I don't know why he's sent it."

"Well, maybe you should catch up with him. How do you look at the moment, are you fat? Oh, doesn't matter. He's seen your back fat from your bra, so maybe he does like you."

I am super-scared at the fact that I might have to be brave.

"Hey, I don't have back fat!"

"Sure you do! We all have it. It's no biggie – it's just bra strap fat. You know the bits. Lift up your shirt and turn around – I'll screenshot it."

"I'm not lifting my shirt up, plus, I've been eating a shit ton of kale and mushrooms and I've lost a bit of weight. Anyway, what do I do, do I send a text back?"

"Probably just as well – where are you? The lighting is terrible. Why aren't you in front of a window? You should get your colours done and get some good foundation."

"Workshop, overhead fluoros, yes, the lighting is terrible. Don't like foundation. Anyways... Help meeeeeeee! This stuff is hard."

"Why don't you give him some options – like choose a Friday and a Monday next week. Then if you catch up sooner, you will know. Either way, it will put an end to the doubt. You will have an answer and can move forward instead of being stuck. Come on, Belle. Sitting and wondering isn't being brave or vulnerable. Actually putting your fucking self out there and finding out is being vulnerable. You and I both know you need to move forward, and then you will know, one way or another, whether this guy likes you or not. You will know."

"Okay. Good idea. Gosh, I miss the tech-free date days with pubs in my twenties. So how's the whole girl crush thing working out?"

"Ooh, I'm coming over in November. You can meet her. I've been watching some YouTube videos. And I've been researching and, you know, finding out all the different terminologies. I'm definitely a lipstick lesbian. Birdie would be a chapstick. But I'm having to face my own body issues now as she is really super-fit, like yoga fit, and I'm, well, you have seen where my boobs hang. If they could sing they'd sing 'Swing Low Sweet Chariot'. Hahaha."

I burst out laughing. "I'd love to meet her. So do you think you are gay or bi, or is it person-specific?"

"I think it's person-specific. But if I listen to my heart and gut, I reckon we will get married."

"Oh, yay! I want to be bridesman or bestmaid or whatever. Either way, I want to wear a suit like Carrie Bradshaw did in the *Sex and the City* movie, and everything. I'm so coming to your wedding. Alright. Let me think about what to text Baker. Gotta run. I need to pack up and get home. I want to catch a wave before the sun goes down. Keep you posted."

After my late-afternoon surf, I text Baker back with some options. It's a Tuesday, so the kids are with their dad – no chance of Abby listening out for phone pings.

Me: *Hey, we could meet at the beach for a walk, or we could meet at Gordon St Garage, or a café on your side. I'm free Thursday afternoon if that works for you.*

I don't want to sit and stare at the phone.

My nerves and curiosity are heightened. Is it possible that maybe someone like him could like someone like me? Was this just a friend-type thing of someone wanting to catch up? Confusion is by far the worst place to be. Clarity is much nicer. Confusion just leads to unhealthy head games, and they are something I am trying to avoid. I am trying to be kind to me. But I am also trying to be brave for me. Balancing the vulnerability with keeping my self-worth and some type of boundary that doesn't suffocate anything is really hard.

It's new ground, even catching up for a chat, and man am I struggling to find my footing. Hiking the canyon was easier. I wish a sinkhole would appear in my kitchen right now and suck my anxiety down into its pit. That would be nice.

I put my phone in the fridge where my chocolate stash normally hides from the kids. The fridge now holds bunches of kale, avocados, mushrooms and tomatoes. Don't have to worry about that being hidden from the kids.

Trying to distract myself works for about an hour as my wardrobe gets a clean-out. Tunes get cranked. Snapchat karaoke takes place. What on earth has my life become! I mean, I'm literally trying to avoid staring at my phone, willing dots to appear that signal a response. Not exactly what I had pictured my 43-year-old self to be doing on a Tuesday night. I do my best to avoid the phone, and finally cave somewhere around 8:37ish.

I pick up the phone. Three missed FaceTime calls from Jo. A

confirmation text from Becs for training in the morning. And Baker. A text from Baker.

Bakes: *Hey, Belle! How about we meet over at the Shorehouse in Swanbourne on Thursday afternoon about 3?*

Shit. Fancy-ish. Well, no more fancy than Gordon St Garage, I guess. I just need to remember ballet flats and play it cool.

Me: *Perfect! See you then.*

The catch-up for coffee over near his studio to talk adventures and just general life stuff is set. And once again, I do my best to daggy on down. As much as you can daggy on down for a beachside café in Swanbourne, anyway. Play it cool. Keep myself guarded.

He lets me know that he has shut his business down and is returning to teaching. He's returned to the job that made him miserable.

"Why did you do that?" I ask.

"Well, I thought maybe I should go back instead of being in business full-time. I thought I should try to go after my career in education a little more – it's familiar. But I'm starting to realise that I might have made a mistake. That maybe I should have been braver in starting something new, as opposed to trying to go back and build something where I feel like I give all my energy, without return."

I'm a little shocked. At least my undie anxiety can end. Phew.

"Sooo… does that mean you won't be pincushioning people anymore, and making them feel like a big dork when you ask them personal questions?"

"I don't know yet… I don't know how much energy I will have to give to my business."

I start to wonder if all our chats were weird, two-way coaching sessions where we both learnt something. He certainly was a teacher, he just may not have been in the right space.

"So why did you decide to go back to a space where it's give on one side?"

"I don't know – I like supporting the kids. But my boss has been really hard to deal with. No matter how much I put in, I just can't get to that next level. Seems he is more than happy to let me take on all these projects but never reciprocate any appreciation. So now I don't know what to do. I'm stuck between moving forward and staying and trying to get to the next step."

I think on the pain and anguish I see him in. Crush aside, I feel for him. I don't like seeing people in conflict or pain, and he seems like he is in need of a friend. I really don't want to complicate things for him, despite how much I am wondering if there is a spark. So my poker face stays put, and I think about what I can tell him to help.

"Look, I've worked in enough businesses to know that there is no guarantee with anything. You can choose to stay stuck, or you can choose... Hang on, you teach English, right? There is a poem I know which might help you. I'll find it and send it to you. But don't read it now – read it later."

I grab my phone and search for the poem, and flick it through to him. It reads:

> Caught between the possibility of happiness
> The weighted chains of responsibility,
> What's right may also be what's wrong
> In this life
> Those stories about success that we crafted as we grew
> Those stories now do a disservice
> To the growing, changeling
> You
>
> The leap seems like a canyon; a vast expanse of unknown
> Paralysed you stay together yet disconnected and alone
> What will the future say of you
> and your brave
> That standing still was standing strong
> Opportunities buried before your grave
>
> Call out
> Get help
> Jump
> Take the bloody leap
> That hill, that canyon, that great divide
> Focus on the view you will feel

When happiness, joy, love, worthiness
Are back inside.
~ Anon

"Look, at the end of the day, Bakes, happiness is not a structural thing. You are responsible for your own happiness, and I get that being brave and creating change is scary. It takes time, so be kind to yourself. But I also know that companies can restructure, kids grow up, get jobs, change jobs, so you need to think about what you want to teach your kids about being happy, really. And that is something that doesn't get taught in school. If you want to get to 65 or 70 and say that you lasted 30 or 40 years in teaching – that is an achievement. But if you do that, and you have spent the most part of your life deeply unhappy, then what? I've got three dead family members. Life is short. You don't need a lot, but you do need to be happy – and going after that takes real bravery, because you might fail. You might get hurt."

"Did you eat Yoda for breakfast?"

"Haha, no. I have just lived a life, and I am trying to be brave. I might fail with what I do, but I will be okay. I'd rather die being brave and trying than be stuck in misery, because I know what that is like, personally and professionally, and it's not good for anyone. I want to teach my kids to go after joy. I want them to know what a life filled with love looks like."

"Love?"

"Love for who they are, what they do, and knowing that they are worthy of other people loving them, too, and seeing their light and brilliance. Anyway... let's change the subject."

"Are you dorking out again?"

"Can you tell? God, I'm so embarrassed. I think heart-based bravery is the hardest one, the most awkward one for a lot of people to embrace. It's just a hunch, but I reckon putting yourself out there on the line, ready to potentially be rejected, would probably be the hardest thing. I mean, it is not the same place as when you and I were in our twenties. There's Tinder, and Tinder judgement, and no one talks to anyone, and there's social media stalking, and expectations and, you know, for some women, our bodies have changed if we've had enormous babies. It's scary. I think it's scary, anyway."

"Even scarier than the frogs?"

"Tougher than that. Tougher than asking for money in work. Tougher than facing fears of sharks or heights or anything. I know I'm super-freakin' scared. Love is scary. Well, for me, especially seeing as I'm wanting to be brave and put myself back out there."

He stares at me intently – those blue eyes. That hair. Shit. What am I even doing sitting here? I don't know where to look, so I look down at my plate and fidget with the smoked salmon, wishing I was anywhere else. I wish I was a Tic Tac back in the Grand Canyon right now.

There is a big pause, and as I look up, I watch his face get heavy with the weight of his predicament. He looks at the smoked salmon on my plate, and switches gears. I think he does this to stop the progress, that maybe fear is getting to him. I understand. I'm being scared now. I may never get my answer to whether he likes me or not.

"I don't like smoked salmon – it grosses me out."

"Oh? Okay. Well, lucky you didn't order it then. So, look, I hope you figure out what to do… I get that moving forward is hard, but staying in unhappiness is much, much worse. Just be kind to yourself, okay? You are a good guy, no matter what you think you have done or haven't done. You can't get your boss to do what you want. Your happiness is up to you and your choices."

He hugs me and we say our goodbyes. Inside I am a little disappointed, and a little happy. That seems to be the end of the crush. It seems that he just needed advice. So I try to shake the feeling that I like him, and think about moving on.

I hop in the car and FaceTime Jo to debrief.

"And? What happened? Oh, your boobs look great! Good choice on the black singlet."

"Huh. Thanks, but it doesn't matter, Jo. He just needed advice on what to do with his life, I think. So I am no more clear on whether he likes me, and whether there is an attraction or not. But, just to debrief you, you know me – I have treated any time that I catch up with him as one where I don't put any effort in and I try to daggy on down a little bit so that he doesn't think anything of me, and that I am not putting anything at risk. So, I figured just plain black singlet is okay. And yeah, that is the upside to me carrying a bit of extra weight – my boobs do look amazing. They will disappear though."

I have, by my own judgement, about 15 kilos to lose still, but it has been dropping off since I made the decision that I deserve a banging hot bod – only because that is where I know I feel my absolute rockstar best. Except it's a trade-off: flat stomach, flat chest. Fucking sucks.

"Well, that's shit," says Jo. "But hey, he must like you, even with you being fat. How were you brave, then? Belle, you are still in the same position you were months ago – wondering whether he likes you or not."

"Yeah, but he has a lot going on, and I don't want to add any complication."

"But what about your own complications? You are making you less important than other people again. You can't keep doing that. You are not being kind to you."

My beautiful, honest friend gets straight to the point. She is so right. I have once again repeated that pattern of lowering my own value in relationships.

"I know… I'll get there; when the time is right, I'll get there and be okay. Look, I've gotta get home. I'm going to try and fit a surf in tomorrow morning after school drop-off. I'll speak with you soon."

"Hey, before you go, get yourself a vibrator. You'll feel better."

"Jo, I've been okay until now. It's really not a priority."

"Just do it, okay – but don't buy the one called the rabbit, it will ruin penises for you forever. It's too good."

"Thanks for the review. I've really got to go… Bye!"

That evening, I get a text from Bakes: *Thanks for catching up with me. You are an inspiring person, Belle.*

Oh, yay me, I think sarcastically. I mean, I do love helping people. I'm just getting to a point where it would be so nice if a man thinks I'm awesome and amazing and, dare I say, dateable, loveable, all the 'ables', and makes me the one who gets got – not the one who is inspiring, or who got away. But where it's reciprocated – not where they are a stalker or anything. Because, hey, it needs balance. Just like Jo said. Oh, shit. I have to be brave.

I reply with kindness, as I can't help liking him. Still. I have tried not to. And if he were attractive with a douche personality, it would be easier to not like him at all. But I like the banter. I've liked the stupid chats about whether you'd rather face off against a crocodile or a shark.

Me: *Bakes, at the risk of sounding like a bumper sticker, keep being brave – you'd be amazed at the cool stuff you can do. Just give yourself permission.*

Bakes: *Thanks, I'm hoping some of your braveness rubs off on me. I'm starting to believe.*

Me: *Well, I know a good place to sit and ask the universe for some answers. I just don't recommend crawling to the edge of my rock if you are unco like me...*

Bakes: *It's definitely a good place to start – asking the universe for some direction and clearing the mind.*

I think back to Becs telling me to go and dunk myself in the ocean during summer. It has become a ritual for me to go clear my mind. To disconnect and reconnect. It definitely helps.

Me: *Good idea. Rock, ocean, front lawn... all good spots to clear the mind. But the rock in the Grand Canyon, for me – that takes the cake.*

Bakes: *Awesome. I'll definitely be giving it a try.*

Me: *Well, I've got a plane to catch... literally. Take care of you.*

Bakes: *Thanks, Belle. I like our chats.*

I head out for a surf on Friday morning, looking for my spot on the beach to get out and practise. It's busy this morning thanks to the offshore breeze and some nice, steady sets. There must be at least 40 guys scattered along 200 metres – no hiding my ability today. Most are out the back, a few are in the waist-deep water where I will be. One woman walks past me with a cheery, "Hello! How good is it this morning!" She has a white shortboard tucked under her arm, Ugg boots, and a towel-poncho hybrid-type style going on, with a short, black steamer wetsuit peeking out from under her poncho, ready to strip off and head out.

"Yeah, pretty busy, hey. Will see how I go! I'm Belle, by the way."

"I'm Kat! Nice to meet ya! You been surfing long?"

She looks at my giant yellow board, smiling, as she spikes her board in the sand before stripping off her Ugg boots and poncho.

"Nah, I've just started to learn this year. Got a way to go before I'd feel comfortable on a board like yours! But I love being out there. It's fun."

"Oh, good on ya! Keep going. She's so good for the soul, hey! A good teacher."

"Yeah, just need to keep getting back out there really. I just feel like I shouldn't be here sometimes – but I know sticking it out is the only way I'll get better."

"Ah! Sometimes people forget where they started. But you look like the kinda chick who will keep at it. See ya out there!"

"Enjoy!"

I watch her get on her board, no wet-fish flopping in her style, and head out to the back breaks before catching a beautiful wave and carving it up. You can almost feel her freedom and joy from the shoreline.

I look down at my toes, ready to head out to the breaks at the sandbar, the ones closer to shore. As I hit the tideline, I write a little secret between me and the earth in the wet sand with my big toe, 'Be brave', and I draw a heart around it. The green lady comes and takes it with her, holding my commitment.

I move forward, feeling the change in the water, that feeling of being alive. I promise the green lady that I'll allow my heart to be open again – I'll be brave before the year ends. Plus, I'm running out of things to do on my bravery list. Except for maybe nude yoga, because the body-love issues are still hanging over my head.

The Asia trip is tomorrow. My son wants to try eating a scorpion on a stick. I'm liking that the kids are developing their own bravery in little ways, too.

9

SEPTEMBER

*A*hhh, injuries. In Thailand, I work hard at running on the treadmill and keeping my surf practice up. I eat more som tam (a spicy green papaya salad) while I am there than you could poke a chopstick at. I'm pretty pleased with the progress the bod is making. But the injuries remind me that I am not 28 anymore. I really need to stretch more – I just don't. Deep down, I feel myself going, 'Ah, rats! You have to go see Baker when you land to get your back sorted yet again.' Always an upside to pain, I tell myself.

I text from Thailand hoping Baker is still seeing a few clients as a side hustle. Lucky for me, I score a spot and book in for when I return the following week.

Thursday. Ballet drop-off. Back maintenance. Baker. Once again, the banter is great. Yet, once again, my back is not the only thing that is probed due to discomfort.

"So, tell me about your adventures!"

"Well, I was a little limited at the end of the week because of having issues with my back. It's really frustrating. But I did learn a little bit about myself. Have you been to any parts of Asia before?"

"No. Where did you go?"

"The kids and I started in Singapore to see a friend of mine, Robyn. They knew we were going to Thailand, but I pranked them and said that we'd missed our flight. I surprised the kids with a little trip to Universal Studios."

"Oh cool! How do you go travelling with the kids by yourself?"

"It was one of those mindset things I had decided to do. I didn't want the fact that I'm a single mum to stop me getting out and travelling and doing things. I wasn't sure how I'd go with the kids on rides, but it all worked out."

"What's next on the list, then?"

"I want to go and do Karijini Gorge… I don't even own a tent, though, so that will be a challenge. I don't really care about what I do, I just like being out, local or global – there is so much beauty in the world."

"And what about *you*, are you making space for different adventures this year?"

"What do you mean?"

"Well, are you still single?"

Once again, I feel awkward at the conversation. I don't know whether he likes me or not, but I know I need to move forward.

"Yes, no holiday romances if that's what you mean…"

"Annnd would you be making space for someone?"

I stare at his feet, at his blue trainers that are slightly scuffed on the toes. This is not the first time I've had this question. And you cannot read anything into staring at feet in shoes. Once again, I'm back to wondering what the heck is going on. Confusion sucks balls.

"Ahhh, that's kind of personal. Why are you asking?"

"Just curious."

"Well, yes, I am. It's something I'm trying to do."

"You must get asked out all the time."

"Nope. Not once."

"Reaaally? Why is that?"

"Well, I work with 98 percent women, then I'm busy doing the mum thing, and the house thing, so I guess I'm just not in the space to make it happen. I'm trying to change that, though."

There is a pause as he moves around the table and adjusts the needles in my back.

"So," I ask, "do you make everyone feel this awkward with personal questions on the table, or am I just lucky?"

"Sorry – I don't mean to make you uncomfortable, I'm just curious. That's all."

"Dude, I'm already uncomfortable with pain in my back. We've talked about this before. I'm kinda stuck. I can't read body language staring at the floor. Can we change the subject, please?"

"Okay, what do you want to talk about?"

I try to pop my head up to see if I can make eye contact with him. Oh, no! It's eye-crotch contact, and I almost nose him right in the groin. Like a freaked-out turtle, I retreat back into the hole on the table.

"Well, how are things going with your boss and being back at the college? I appreciate you fitting me in for an appointment. Nice to know you still have time on a Thursday."

As much as I'm not in a position to read any body language, I am quite tuned in and connected to the shift in energy in the room. I sense him internalising his struggles. It's confirmed by a sigh and a hand that then rests on my top right shoulder. I watch the weight on his feet shift from left to right.

"Look, it's not ideal. I'm working my butt off for my boss again, and he is still really happy for me to do all the development work, and take all my ideas to the board, and just leave me with nothing but an empty emotional tank. There is no recognition. No thanks. I think he's happy to have me there but doesn't want to work at helping me get to my goals. I think I need to be brave. I need to work out how to move forward, and it may be by coming back into my business full-time, or it may be by going and working for another school somewhere else. Maybe if I rub your shoulder, some of your braveness will rub off. Haha."

I wish, I think. I just gulp and try to stay cool. "Don't worry, it's all baby steps. I mean, I still have stuff to be brave with. There are plenty of scary things for me to do."

"Like what?"

As I talk, I can feel the needles being removed from my back and know that the session is close to wrapping up.

"I'm facing selling my house, and downsizing, and potentially moving between the coast and the city to help my daughter with her dance dreams. That is scary. I'd be starting over. Again. I have a little network here. But to be honest, I like simple, and I hate driving. It's a waste of time. I'd rather downsize and be minimal – an apartment with enough storage for surfboards, boogie boards, bikes and paddleboards, oooh and then a little hobby farm near the coast to grow vegies and write and drink red wine for the weekends. And fainting goats. They are sooo funny. I love goats. But I'd need to import those. That's the dream. More living, less existing, I say."

"Well, don't move just yet – I like getting to know you."

Cue confusing awkward silence, and my 'what the fuck'-face-in-the-hole routine. I'm going to need Botox soon to stop the rampant 'what the fuck'-face expression lines. You know, the frown lines right in the middle. Confusion is not good for the complexion.

"Well, we are done. I'll leave you to get dressed."

I stand up, still confused by this man. He is way out of my league physically. But is there something there or not?

"So, do you have any clients now?" I ask, instead of what I should be asking.

"Nope, you are the last one for the day."

"Well, hopefully this does the trick. Thanks for your help. I appreciate it."

As I walk out the door of his studio, the breeze catches me. I stop for a second and contemplate my bravery. I wonder if I should go back and say something, and then think better of it.

I start to walk towards the gate. Stop again, and turn and go back.

I knock on the sliding door and, once again, my stomach flips. My heart races, and I attempt to be brave. He opens the door, with that same breeze catching his sandy hair and blowing it back, before he checks his wrists for a hair tie.

"Hey, Bakes. Have you got a minute?"

"Sure – if I can have the hair tie on your wrist?"

"Okay, fair trade."

I take the hair tie off my wrist – I tend to always have one floating around in case my hair gets to me – and pass it to him. He pulls his hair back into a half man bun and smiles.

"So, what's up?"

"Well, oh, okay. I um, okay. Be brave, Belle."

He stares at me, not knowing what to think.

"Look, all our chats have pushed me to be brave this year, and at times they have been really uncomfortable. I've never felt so awkward before so I wanted to say thank you for pushing me outside my comfort zone. I'm still not there yet, but I just thought I'd let you know that I appreciate you creating a safe space so that I can be awkward and ask questions."

"What do you mean?"

"Well, you know, like when I had to be brave and ask about whether you thought I was a corporate bitch, or dressed like a lesbian?"

He chuckles and looks me directly in the eyes.

"Don't take this the wrong way, but I think you're beautiful. I've learnt a bit from our talks, too."

I don't know exactly how to take that comment. Does that mean not interested? Why say it? I thought there was only one way to take that comment.

"What have you learnt, then?"

"Well, that it's hard to be brave. But you inspire me to try to be braver."

I start to blush. I can feel this happening as I don't ever bother with make-up. For a couple of reasons: one, it would just end up stuck all over the face hole; two, I've always preferred not to wear foundation; and three, I certainly didn't want to look like I had made any effort at all. Like, zero. Effort means interest. I'm holding my feelings close to my chest. Poker-style.

"Are you blushing?"

"Yes. I have a love-hate relationship with the word 'inspiring'. I like that I inspire people, but I really don't like if they don't take any action, as then it feels like, *Oh, yay, I had zero impact, really.* Look. At the end of the day, we are responsible for our own happiness. If someone else contributes to it, then it's a bonus. Anyway, thanks for the chat."

On that note, I get a hipster fist bump, and know that it's time to leave.

The next day I end up feeling totally vulnerable. I look at my road ahead going, *Well, I'm not sure what to do.* I'm tormenting myself with mind games and shitty inner self-pity chit-chat.

After years of thinking I had the mindset stuff down pat, at my core, I am still human. Which means, luckily, beautifully, painfully… I can still feel.

This is a good thing, really. It still catches me by surprise in terms of self-bravery and biting the awkward bullet. I know I need to go level 10.

I'm all set to just get him out of my head and enter the world of online dating. The world that is making me cringe. Except, every time I try to set up an account, something stops me. I look at it and think, *I don't want to do this.*

How can you, Belle? You have a stupid crush on Baker and still have no fucking idea if the feeling is mutual? What. A. Chicken.

I let things be. Almost.

The new moon is coming around in a week, and I've started thinking of the bravery circle from the Grand Canyon every time the moon hits new or full. It's become a reminder of what I'm starting, and what I'm finishing each month. It's made me way more conscious that I still have not put myself out there in heart land. Times' a tickin. I'm running out of 2018.

Becs has taught me that new moons are good for manifesting good things. Plus, I'm loving getting in the ocean. Something about it just feels so cleansing. I've learnt a fair bit about her beliefs this year. All these planets in retrograde and eclipse doorways. I find it all interesting. I think I find it interesting because if the moon can control the tides, what else do the other planets influence that science has not caught up to as of yet? Just because we can't see it or have the technology to measure it, doesn't mean that it doesn't exist. I'm kid-free that weekend, so a Friday evening new moon dip seems like a good idea.

Even though the coast forecast is super-fresh and super-choppy, I still think it's a good idea to go do some in-the-sea soul searching. I figure Becs will be down for a dip, so I call her.

"Hey, Becs! Wanna come dunk yourself in the tit-freezing ocean with me next Friday? I'm up for some new moon manifesting. You in?"

"Hey, sure! Why not. I finish a beachside boot camp at 5:30 pm. How about we meet at 6:00 pm? Do you want to grab a wine after?"

"I'll pass on the wine, thanks, gorg. I'm sticking to my clean eats for now.

Happy to have a mineral water, though. Can we just have the drink at the beach?"

"Sounds perfect. See you then."

The new moon rolls around, and off to the beach I go to meet Becs. With a wardrobe inspired by Kat the surfer, my attempt to be all surfer-chick cool does not translate that well. I end up looking like a weird homeless person-slash-couture fashion runway show that I don't understand. Outfit? Bits of all the bulk buys at Aldi. Dried-seaweed-brown striped, picnic rug-style poncho. Black snow boots. Yoga tights with bright orange flame trees printed on a lime-green background. A black bikini throw dress. New black bikini – because the old bikini has become a nudity risk in the ocean. Eclectic dressing: not a look I have mastered today. My chesticles are about to turn into icicle tits. I check myself in the car window and think, *Ah, fuck it, who cares anyway.* I go and sit on the park bench to wait for her, watching the parking lot.

I spot her little blue Mazda, and she waves. Getting out of the car, Becs is in her normal rock god squad cool state. Some people just make trackie pants and a hoodie look hot. I make trackie pants look like I mugged a male accountant who's three inches shorter than me while he was out on a midday park run. It's why I don't own them. Leggings, yes. Jeans, yes. Trackies, nope. Refuse to wear them. Although they may have been a better choice than my current get-up.

The beach is pretty much deserted except for mounds of seaweed that have landed on the white sand from stormy and crazy-arse windy weather. We have been experiencing the kind of wind that if you stood there butt naked in the sand, you'd get a really good exfoliating. Not that I am recommending sandblasting your stretch marks or any other skin, but that's what beach wind gets like here. Our west coast wind is named the Fremantle Doctor. More like Fremantle Microdermabrasion today.

In we go. The water is not as cold as I thought it would be. Probably because in my life pre-kids when I did triathlons, I braved St Kilda Beach for after-work training sessions. At winter's end. When actual ocean-swimming brain freeze happens despite wearing a wetsuit and two swimming caps. This? This is a cakewalk.

We stay waist deep. The sun is setting, so it's really pretty. Rough and pretty. The goal is to manifest, not die. We duck-dive down.

"So, what are your good intentions that you want to bring in?" Becs asks.

"I'm going to focus on making space for someone and welcoming in positive, happy people who might, *MIGHT*, just see the good things about me and I about them. You?"

"I'm going to focus on having booked-out bootcamps and receiving money up front instead of cancellations and no cash."

My friends are really good like that. Being open to their own kind of brave. We have been, and are, each other's cheer squad for feeling the awkwardness of fear and doing it anyway.

"I'm thinking about venturing into the world of online dating. You know, setting myself up on a dating website and getting back out there and being brave. Letting love back in. And I am scared shitless."

"You can do it, Belle. Heaps of people meet that way now."

"You know, Becs, I love how the kick in the pants from you at the start of the year that sent me into the ocean has turned out. It's like you magically healed the relationship between the green lady and me. Now we hang out again. Respect."

"No problem, chick. Make sure you keep at it."

We stay in the ocean for about 10 minutes, before our back-of-the-car drinks and goodbyes. I hop in my car, crank a little old-school RNB Fridays on iTunes and arrive home feeling all fired up. A quick shower, trusty PJs and I'm all set for lounge and laptop time.

Hellooo, dating site. Again. Probably the 23rd time I have looked at it and thought, *I really should do this.* I just haven't.

Internal chit-chat fires up, with my head and heart starting a late-night debate.

Heart: *Why are you doing this? The person that you like is not even on here.*

Head: *Oh, come on. Move on, already. Now is not the right time to be brave and talk to Baker. You are friendzone material. Stay safe! Don't complicate things. Let's just do this online dating thing, okay? It's like a personality quiz. Quizzes are good! Nerds rule. It'll be fine.*

Heart: *Oh, I'm sorry! Guess the whole 'Hey, let's be brave' thing got lost in the heartland of memory – what is it, hippo-something region?*

Head: *Hippocampus.*

Heart: *Guess the reptilian part of your brain has performed a coup. 'Cause now we're all scaredy. Remember the word courage comes from 'coeur', which is French for 'heart'. And French is the language of love.*

Head: *Amygdala coup! You are right. I remember.*

To settle the internal battle, I go back to my trusty early-twenties backpacking decision-making method of flipping a coin. Heads: do the thing. Tails: don't do the thing. If I get one answer and start going 'best of three', then that is a good indication that I am either (a) really chickening out, or (b) know the other option is the one I really want to do.

Building up to the 'do I say anything or not say anything' coin flip is, for me, preceded by a round of fuckfuckfuckfuckfuckfuckityfuckfuck. My swearing is audible.

I'm out of brave things to tick off the list. Now it's scary. Time to really walk my walk. Yes, there is strength in vulnerability. There is also strength in tequila and red wine. But being not much of a drinker, there is none on hand. Self-talk activated.

"Right, Belle. Ladyballs up and move on. Make your friends proud. Clarity comes from courage. Soon, you will know."

I make a plan. Plans have helped before. I switch to notes on my laptop and jot down some points.

1. Do I care about the outcome (because sometimes the unknown is a dangerous comfort zone – ha! That's totally getting turned into a quote)?
2. Who might have a different take on this?
3. Is there something else scary I can do first?

Yes, I care about the outcome. I will actually know. This is scary. Maybe it's scary because I know that 'happy ever after' doesn't work out. He is the first person who has caught my attention since I became single. I've navigated the kids conversations. I've worked on being kind to me, even though I could still be kinder.

Hector might have a different perspective. A guy perspective would be good. I know he's been dating. He sits high on the honesty scale.

As for the scary thing? I haven't told Becs about my crush. I've toyed with confiding for quite some time, but then get too scared to say anything and just let it slide. She knows I am trying to set up this online dating thing. Arrrgh!

Okay, trusty coin-flipping decision-making process, here goes…

I get up and scour the house for a coin. You can never find a coin when you need one. Unless you have been travelling and have random currencies from different parts of the world lying in the drawer where your passport lives. Then you can find plenty. Opening up the wooden drawer… jackpot. Yay for keeping the 'in case you win a trip and need your passport pronto' drawer organised.

Take your pick, Belle. US nickel, 10 Thai baht, Singapore dollar, pound sterling, franc, euro, Vietnamese dong, New Zealand 20-cent piece.

10 Thai baht it is.

Heads: I'll tell Becs.

Tails: I'll not say anything and just leave things as-is.

Aaand it comes up heads. Shit. Time to ladyballs up.

I wander back out to the lounge, where my phone and laptop are parked. A little more procrastination and fear feeding.

I stare at the dating site, tapping my fingers on the top of the screen.

Some of it is fairly straightforward. Other parts, I honestly have no idea what the hell things mean, or what to choose.

I mean, let's start with the layout. My gender (female) seeking (male). Fairly straightforward. Right underneath the seeking is 'height'. Wait, website – do you mean my height or the height I'm seeking, because that is pretty specific. My height. Okay. Fine.

Then the 'I am looking for a':

This is where I start going, *I don't bloody know…*

Is 'hang out' code for 'pick up'? Wouldn't you just start with hanging out? Where's the line between a date and hanging out?

Or why would I be 'looking for friends'? If I was looking for friends, why would I only need to choose 'seeking male friends'? By friends do they mean 'special friends' or platonic friends? What type of friend?

Then there is 'dating'. Well, that seems like the obvious choice. But does that mean people who might want to go on a date with me would not be open to being friends if it doesn't work out?

And then, even scarier… 'long term'. Ultimately, that is the goal. Seems pretty serious to put all that pressure on something so early on. What if the long-term people are stalkers? What if they are stage five cling-ons?

Why can't it just say 'dating'? I'll choose dating.

I start hitting snags.

'Body type': Thin, athletic, average, a few extra pounds, BBW. Wait, website – WTF is BBW? I don't even know what that means! How many extra kilos is a few? Like, five or 25? I wouldn't say I'm thin; average, maybe? I don't bloody know.

I'll park that one and ask Becs about it. Either Becs or Google. One of them is sure to know. Definitely Google, but Becs probably has some knowledge on this stuff.

Skip that question…

'Do you want children?' What do you mean? I already have children. Do I want the children I already have? Of course, I love my kids!

Do I want other peoples' children? Do I want more children of my own?

Honestly, this is just turning into a big fuckfuckityfuck of a dumb idea that I don't really want to do anyway.

Maybe I should just take up triathlon again. No – that takes up too much time.

I persevere with the site…

Some questions are a little more straightforward, lucky for me.

'Drugs?' No.

'Smoke?' No.

'Drink?' On occasion. Not a daily occasion, just actual occasions. But not really a drinker.

'Religion?' New age? Am I new age? What is a new-age religion? Like, that I believe in a bit of universal woo? I believe in God? I don't worship any weird trees or anything. I'm not a Jedi. I like Buddhism, but I'm not a practising Buddhist. I wouldn't say non-religious because I believe in stuff – I just don't really have a team. Bit like football – I appreciate the game, I just haven't been to a game in a while. Okay. 'Spiritual' will do… who knows.

Through that hurdle. Next hurdle. 'Describe your personality in one word.' After all the deliberation on kids, religion and body type, I'm expecting to choose 'neurotic overthinker'.

The list is extensive. Oh, shitola.

Starting with 'Adventurer' seems like a good fit. I like adventures. 'Animal lover' – yes, but not to the point that I want to dress like my dog on purpose. 'Beach bum', 'Blogger', 'Blue collar'. How are these personality types? Who made this website?

With a whole gamut of gems in here from 'Brogrammer' – *WTF is a Brogrammer?* – through to 'Princess' (I kinda get it – so not me), 'Starving Artist' (dates will not involve food there), 'Player' (up-front and honest, nice), 'Sapiophile'* (*WTF? Clearly I'm not one of those or I'd know what it means*), the second-last one takes the cake.

'Vegan.'

Since when is vegan a personality type? I mean, come on. Could you imagine? Here's a potential conversation with my good friend Becs.

"Hey, Becs. If you were to describe my personality, would you use the word vegan?" Note, I'm not a vegan. I like vegan food, and would be 83 percent vegan, but I also like ice-cream and occasional bacon in my world.

How do you describe a vegan personality? Do vegans make jokes? Do they not smile? Do they smile all the time? I know three vegans. Two of them say, "That's funny" but they don't laugh. Come to think of it, none of them have told me a joke. Anyways...

At this stage, the more scary, more awkward, more immediate action of crush confession seems a little more doable.

Time to call Becs. Here goes. Phone at the ready. I call her.

"Hey, Becs, I've taken the plunge. I'm trying to set this stupid online dating account up. I don't even know what BBW means... I'm stuck."

"Why do you think you are stuck?"

"Well... I might have a crush on someone."

"Is it... me?"

"Shit, no. No offence."

"Oh... okay. 'Cause you know I'm gay, right?"

"Uh, yeah. Of course. You know I'm not, right?"

"Yeah – I'm just messing with you!"

I hear her thinking through the phone.

"Sooo is this person someone that I know?"

"Ummm. Yes."

"And are you going on a dating site so that this person might realise you are back dating again, and maybe realise that you are available?"

Sheepishly high pitched, "Yes..."

"And... why are you not telling this person that you like them?"

"Gah. Two reasons. One, despite crowing like a rooster about bravery, I'm more chickenshit than I thought. I'm scared of getting hurt. And two, I don't think the timing is right for them."

"What if this person likes you back?"

"Well, I don't know if they do, because I am confused."

"Is this person an ex?"

"Nope! Not an ex. But you do know them. It's, um, Baker."

"Hahaha. Okay. Keep going and set up the account, and maybe he will find out, but you can't sit there and do nothing. I won't say a word. See you in the gym Monday."

"I know... *sigh*. Thanks for the chat. Love you heaps babes."

Arrrgh.

I start pacing around the house in my PJs, looking at the time and wondering if I should do anything or nothing.

Back to the computer, stare at the screen. Pick up the dog. Put down the dog. Pace some more. Utter shit fuck fuckity fuck.

The self-talk kicks in, as my head and heart keep wrestling with each other, only to be adjudicated by gut intuition.

Come on, Belle. You can be brave. You can do this. Think of all the stuff you have gone through in your life. This is just another notch in the belt of awkward for you. You are about to get your awkward black belt, kimosabe.

I pick up my phone, and I start to type a text to Baker. I feel sick. Then I actually go and throw up. Nerves.

I persevere.

I re-read the text. Start safely, in the shallows. And hit send.

Me: *Hey Bakes. Thanks for the chat the other day. I've been swimming in the ocean with Becs. Did you ever end up doing some soul-searching and asking the universe for a little more clarity?*

Bakes: *Yeah, I have been. It's sooo good.*

Me: *Well, I have loved my ocean swims. I didn't love it so much when I got home and had no hot water. Ummm. I'm going to try to be brave and do one more scary thing on my list.*

Bakes: *What's the last thing? I thought you'd done them all with sitting on rocks in canyons, and touching frogs and all the other things you have been working on this year.*

Me: *Not quite. Well... I am about to become one of those weirdo online dating people we have talked about. It's either that or I think I might face an old lady death of being eaten by a thousand apartment cats. And I have a terrible crush that I need to put to bed in the friendzone.*

Bakes: *You don't need online dating, you will find someone through your adventures. But is the last scary thing joining online dating, or putting the crush into the friendzone? And if you have a crush, why are you friendzoning them?*

I stare, thinking about what to say.

Me: *Both... because.. I don't want to add any more complexity to their life.*

Bakes: *For someone who likes chatting with needles in their back, you are being very vague today.*

Me: *Okay fine. Fuck.*

Bakes: *???*

Me: *I have a crush on you and have no idea through all our little chats if you feel the same, or if you have those types of chats with everyone or if you think the same way about me so friendzoning you seems like the right thing to do given you have so much going on with your work situation and sorting through that conflict.*

There is an awkward pause, as I watch the little grey thinking dots.

Me: *There, said it. Still vague?*

Another awkward pause. I might vomit. Again. I sit staring at the grey 'I'm getting a text back' dots while I wonder what is going on. I feel sick, stupid and like I have just signed up to be the first live crash test dummy – only to realise the magnitude of what I have just done to my heart, and my vulnerability. I pick up my phone, stare at it. Put it back down. Pick it up. Still thinking dots.

I let out an audible "aaaargh". Shit fuck fuckity fuck. There goes the good acupuncturist, Belle. Why didn't you just get online? Ohmygodohmygodohmygod, what have you done? Why does this feel worse than when I was 18? Have you been brave or stupid? Too late now – it's out. God, I'm gonna puke.

The dots start taunting me, like some uppity three-balled digital caterpillar that knows a secret about you that you don't know. You know, like when a person is typing and deleting and typing and deleting, and you know it's not a long text but a short text – you feel it in your guts.

Bakes: *Belle, you are so brave. I couldn't have done that. But why don't we catch up next week and you can tell me in person and we'll see what happens. No, not vague. You blew my mind.*

Me: *I honestly might vomit.*

Me: *Okay. I'll just stay confused for a few more days.*

Bakes: *Don't be confused. I like you. We should chat about things, though, given our locations and work situations.*

Me: *I know. Hence the friendzone and being respectful.*

Bakes: *Thank you, and I really do appreciate that, but let's not friendzone. Not just yet.*

To say that I feel like I am going to vomit a bunch of Sundays is an understatement. I am totally freaking out.

Pick up pick up pick up. I stare at my phone as I wait for Jo to answer her FaceTime call.

"Hey, what's happening? I've only got five minutes. I'm driving back from Hobart. I've been out. I'm about to hit a forest."

"It won't take long. I did it. I told him I have a crush on him."

"Hot Hands?"

"Yep. I did it. Now I think I'm going to be sick." I relay the text conversation to her.

"When are you catching up?"

"Next Thursday. At the beach. For a walk. I'm freaking out. Jo. Jo? Are you there?"

Stupid Telstra network. Stupid forest. Right at the crisis point. I wait 15 minutes and call her again.

Come on, Telstra, get my bestie back on the line.

She answers.

"Sorry; forest. So, what's happening?"

"Next few days, we are catching up at the beach. I'll let you know. Hey, when are you here?"

"First week of October. See you then. Ring me! I'm proud of you. You did it. Yaaay!"

I wait until we catch up. I wait for my safe space, hoping that safe space is going to be delivered with kindness and honesty and a killer pair of biceps.

10

OCTOBER

I feel. Like. An. Idiot. I sit there in the beach car park waiting for him to turn up, twiddling my thumbs. I stare out the window at the ocean and watch the surfers head down to catch the late-afternoon set. There is an offshore breeze blowing. I watch the dance between the surfers and the green lady as I wait to catch up with Baker.

My stomach is in knots. I keep twisting my fingers backwards and forwards and fidgeting with the bracelets on my arm and my two small wave rings, full of nerves. They are looser. I've been dropping the excess weight since August.

I've turned up with hot chocolate. In a thermos. And two cups. With an escape plan. If it all turns to shit, I'll accidentally spill my hot chocolate on myself and go, "Oooh, no, I'd best get going," and scurry away. Which I'm kinda hoping I don't have to do, considering I've finally upped my dress sense and am wearing a purple off-the-shoulder jumper, as the weather is slightly cool, with a grey Bonds singlet underneath. I'd really prefer not to accidentally-on-purpose hot chocolate my new, little-bit-sexy knitted jumper. Maybe it's motivation to be brave.

Maybe he's not turning up. Maybe he's going to ghost me. Ghosting. There's a term I've had to learn. What's the other one I've heard? Catfishing.

Gosh. This whole getting-back-out-there is scary as fuck. But – brave is brave.

His car approaches and parks next to mine. I watch him sit there and stare, and smirk and wave, as he gets out of his car and coolly walks around to open my door.

"Shall we walk down the beach?" he says.

"Sure! I'll just take my shoes off."

Thank goodness I've had a pedicure.

The awkward silence could be cut with a knife. I shove my spare hand into the pocket of my denim shorts as we walk along the sand barefoot until we find a spot to sit in the dunes.

"So," he says, "this is a nice surprise."

More awkward silence. I look at him, holding my breath, before replying. "Well... this is pretty much the last being-brave bit. It's also been nerve-wracking, frustrating, scary, because I have been so confused."

"You are brave, Belle. I couldn't have done what you just did."

He stares at me with those piercing blue eyes. They are the colour of the skyline just above the sea. I can't help but fidget. Fidget and feel like I am going to vomit. Like my heart is actually going to bust out of my rib cage and run screaming into the water by itself, shouting, "Whaaat haaave yooou dooone!" Leaving me sitting there on the beach with a gaping hole in my chest. Trying to catch my breath.

"I don't know. I feel really stupid. But just know, whatever you say, I'm totally cool with it. I just needed to find out before I get back out there. I'd rather live with rejection than regret."

"Well, I do like you, so you haven't imagined it. I think you are amazing. And I'd never have had the guts to tell you. You inspire me to be brave, Belle."

That becomes tick one. I haven't imagined it. Yay for bravery! The heart calms down, as I sit there and wait for the 'but'.

"Do I sense a 'but'?"

He stares out at the ocean, and once again the silence becomes loud and awkward. I can see he is trying to find the right words, trying to still be his kind and courteous self.

"I just don't know how this would work. I'm trying to figure out what to do on the work and business front. There are logistics. I mean, I see you, and you seem to have it all sorted and going on, and I think we could have great adventures together. We both like surfing. You could get rid of scary spiders. I could hide behind you if there is a mugger. You're funny. You make me laugh."

I stare at him, and nervously look up, biting my lip to stop myself saying anything dumb while I absorb what he is saying.

He stares back with that thinking face. The face like when I wore my 'I'm a bit less than my ideal weight' grey dress and felt like he was imagining what the front looked like. You know. Where you can see the glint in someone's eyes, and you can't help but blush.

"Stop looking at me like that!"

He punches me in the arm, knocking me off balance, and I fall over in the sand.

"Oh, sorry!"

I sit up, with half a face of sand. Some of it stuck to my clear lip gloss.

"Pffft." I try to get the sand off.

"Have you got lipstick on?"

"Um, just clear gloss."

"Did you put that on because we were catching up?"

"NO! I always wear clear lip gloss, I just don't wear it when I know I'm going to have my face stuck in a tiny hole and be asked weird questions, weirdo."

I punch him back. He doesn't move. OMG. Those arms.

"Sooo... now what?"

"What's in the thermos?"

Labrador move, I think to myself. His face lights up. Deflect with a tennis ball. Except, the thermos of hot chocolate is the tennis ball.

"Oh – I brought hot chocolate. The good stuff."

"Let's do that first, and then we can think about the so-now-whats."

As we share a hot chocolate, the wind blows up, sand landing in both cups. I should have thought about the cups a bit better. Especially being at the beach – bit gritty. But, upside, at least it's not stuck to my lip gloss anymore.

The wind is causing a little havoc. His mop of surfer curls blows into his face, getting a little caught on his stubble. I mean, could the man be any hotter?

"Pffft." His turn to get hair out of his face.

"Can I have that?" He points to my navy hair tie and grabs it from my wrist.

"Thief! What else are you going to lift?"

"Oh, sorry. But I do like your aviators. They will probably look good on me too." He smiles.

I like wrinkles on a man. It's nice. I think men are lucky in that sense. I don't know if they feel the same pressure as women to stay youthful. Who knows. I'm sure their bodies go through their own challenges as they age.

"So... Thanks for catching up. I know this is weird and awkward and now I'll have to look for another acupuncturist."

"Well, don't find another one just yet. How about we hang out for a bit and, you know, just spend some time where you aren't facedown – oh, this is sounding wrong. Ummm. You know. How about we hang? Like, next Thursday. Could go for a little surf if the conditions are right."

"Ummm, okay. Sure."

"Well, I'm so glad you told me. So. Uh. Ummm..."

Now he is the one looking awkward. He stands up and reaches a hand down to help me up from the sand. As he pulls me up, I bump into him, expecting a hug – the normal kind of goodbye hug after a chat.

But he goes in to kiss me. I stupidly misread it, and it ends up this weird half face kiss. Kind of like when you are dodging your nana who likes to kiss you on the lips but you'd rather not. But he is not my nana. Far from it. Damn. First kiss fail.

"Well. Right. See you next Thursday." I hotfoot it back to my car, leaving Baker behind with the thermos.

"Hey, Belle!"

He catches me at the car. Damn it. The awkwardness continues. As I turn, I can see that he looks just as awkward as me. Doubt that is how he saw the kiss going down either. No one likes a weird nana-style lip-kiss dodge. Nana or no nana. They just aren't good.

"Ummm... here's your thermos. And your hair tie. See you Thursday?"

"Yep. Sure. Thanks, bye."

I'm not quite sure who leaves the car park first. I think it's like an awkward race out of there.

188

"So, come on, tell me. What's happening with Hot Hands? Do you need to broaden your field? Are you going to go on dates? Was it a bust? Did you kiss him?"

Jo's voice is coming out of my phone speaker but I can't quite figure out what I'm looking at as she interrogates me. "Where are you? What am I looking at here?" I ask.

"Well, I was busting for the loo, but I figure you and I can talk like this. There's no secrets between us, really, so don't worry. I'm peeing so that you can't hear me pee."

"What do you mean so I can't hear you pee?"

"Surely you must know this trick? You know!"

"No, I just know I'm staring at the ceiling."

Her face peers over the camera, and I see her long, unruly curls hang forward as she starts to laugh. "You know, how you put your bum towards the front of the toilet bowl so that when you pee it doesn't splash it the water and it trickles down the side so you can't actually hear the pee?"

"Well, I'm not really in the habit of FaceTiming and toilet timing."

"I figured after telling me about that giant crap in Vegas, we are at that level."

"Hahaha. Touché, my friend."

"'Hey, I'm not touché-ing anything." She snort laughs.

"OMG stop, you know your snort laugh makes me laugh!"

We both erupt in giggles until we can contain ourselves. It's a mix of snort laughing and donkey-like hee-hawing with tears streaming.

"Ah – I can't breathe! Jo! Anyway. Ah... I learnt something new. Here's the CliffsNotes. Supposed to catch up again next Thursday. Kiss – ummm, sort of. Totally awkward. Other dates... well, that is to be determined."

"Well, keep me posted. Hey, I'm coming over soon. I want you to meet Birdie. I'm in love. It's kinda nice that we are going through these things at the same time. You know, the love bubble stuff. Well, except for the lesbian bit. But if you decide to broaden the field, at least I'll be able to tell you all about it."

"I've gotta go get the kids from school. I'll update you on Thursday."

When 10:30 pm rolls around, I am lying here thinking about the day's events. I try Netflixing to take my mind off things and get to sleep. Anything with Jason Bateman used to be my go-to for getting off to sleep, as I find the tone of his voice quite soothing for some reason. This was a great strategy until I started feeling guilty about not actually ever making it through any of his shows or movies, and that he might actually be talented. So now here I am, hooked on watching *Ozark*. All because I felt guilty about falling asleep on JB.

I'm staring at my phone, breaking all my rules on watching stuff and having technology right next to me on my pillow, when my phone pings with a text.

Bakes: *Are you awake?*

Me: *Umm. No. Wait, yes. Lol.*

Bakes: *Haha. Just wanted to say was great to see you today, Belle. Ummm. I'd like to redo the weirdness that was at the end if that's okay.*

Me: *Was a bit weird, hey. Sorry – you just caught me by surprise (smiley emoji).*

Bakes: *Guess we are both surprised. I am really glad that you are brave, though.*

Me: *NW.*

Bakes: *NW?*

Me: *No worries. All good. See you next week. Night.*

Ahhh. Baker. Maybe I'll go to sleep thinking about the fact that I might just see him without a shirt on next week. If his hugs are anything to go by, I'm guessing that he is a fairly fat-free zone.

"Mum, why is the surfboard in the car for ballet today?" Abby asks.

"Oh, I just thought I'd go for a little surf at Scarborough while you are at ballet, seeing as the weather is nice. That okay with you, chickeny?"

"Sure. Will you be all wet when you come and pick me up?"

"No, there are showers there, I should be fine. Not sure if I will go in or not, depends on the waves really. I prefer our home beach as I'm not comfortable yet, which just means I'm still learning."

"Oh, okay. Mum?"

"Yes, chickeny?"

"Why do you keep smiling?"

"Oh, it's just a good day, chicken."

"Have you got a date?"

"Why?"

"Well, I want you to know that I am fine now if you do. It was weird when we talked about it, but I'm used to the idea now. Just make sure that they are kind. I think kind is important."

"You are wise beyond your years. And yes, I am catching up with a friend for a surf, but it is early days, so nothing to worry about."

"Will you tell me if you are going to see them again?"

"Yes, chickeny. But for now, just go and enjoy ballet. I'll see you in a few hours."

"Love you, Mum."

"Love you too."

I watch her go into her ballet college. The picture of innocence. Wise beyond her years. I just want her to deal with kid-sized problems, not adult-sized problems, so I stay conscious of what I share with her.

My thoughts turn to meeting Baker at the beach, as I drive over to Scarborough to catch up.

His car is already in the car park. I can see he has two boards in the back. Not sure why, but I can see him sitting there, his hair pulled back in a bit of a man bun. Not like a hipster – I wouldn't place him in the barista-hipster category. More just a free spirit.

I park beside him to see what the go is, and once again watch as he hops out and kind of saunters over. Sooo not like a labrador. More like some kind of jungle sex panther slinky thing. But in a cool, non-sleazy way.

"Hey!" he says. "Thought we'd go for a walk first, and then maybe a surf. I kinda want the backstory."

"Backstory?"

"Yeah! Of you."

"Well, if you want to hear it…"

"Well, I want to know how you got started in your biz, and what happened with your family, and all that kind of stuff, and how you ended up here, basically."

"I'll try to keep it high-level, as some of it is not that great."

As we walk along, I tell him all the details of how I ended up doing what I'm doing, how my mum died, my dad died, my sister died, how my marriage ended, how I've been learning to surf, how I figured out how to have tough conversations, how I learned how to ask for money in business – all of it, basically.

His questions are rapid-fire, interspersed with *I'm going to hold your hand, then not hold your hand, as after last week's weird nana dodge-kiss, I'm not sure if I should hold your hand or not.*

It's a bit tricky to speak coherently with this weird hand-holding/not-hand-holding cha-cha with someone hot.

Walking back, it's my turn for questions. How did you go from teaching to acupuncture? How was the diving with sharks? What else is on your list for brave things to do? How will you choose to be happy when you don't like your job that much? Are you going to laugh at my surfing skills? Where do your mum and dad live? If you wanted to surf anywhere, where would you go? Can you sing?

As we arrive back at the car, I wonder if I am actually going to find out what is beneath the grey T-shirt.

I have been disciplined with eating well, and I'm down 15 kilos since July – almost back at my fighting weight, where I feel good about me. But I'm nervous.

It also means he is going to find out what is beneath my black tank top. Shit. This will be the first time someone I find attractive will have seen me since I was part of a couple. That is a looong time between drinks. Drinks and six-pack abs. Not that I ever had those fully formed, but this will be officially the first time my body – which looks like a cat has used me as its own scratching post – is seen by a hot man. It's nerve-wracking. No amount of self-love has changed the fact that this is still a scary, awkward, I-might-be-rejected-before-anything-even-happens moment.

"You ready to go out for a little surf and show me what you've learned so far this year?"

"I guess so. But no making fun of me – I'm still learning, okay?"

"Promise. Do you want to use my Mini Mal or your big yellow?"

"I'll stick with big yellow. It's kind of my security blanket. Sharks don't eat yellow things, right?"

"Don't know. Can they see colour?"

"I have no idea. I just need to be out of the water before you."

We grab the boards and head down to the water.

"Okay, so I get self-conscious when it comes to this," Baker says. Yes, Baker, *the hot guy*, says.

"Are you kidding! You have not had babies come out of your body and treat your stomach like it was a house party that needed some graffiti to say 'kids were here'. What are you worried about?"

"Oh, I still get self-conscious. It's probably why I try to stay so fit, as I'm worried I don't have big enough muscles. I'm not six foot four or anything. I'm just me. But I'm a happy me, so that's important, right. Do you want to get in the water first, or will you feel better if I do?"

"Oh, after you?"

"Okay then – but you get out first."

"Deal."

"No peeking."

"Okay." *As if!* I watch as he loses his shirt and strips down to his boardies, taking his surfboard into the shallows and paddling out. I'm worried I'm in over my head here. While these waves look nice, I'm a little worried about someone other than Surf Dundee watching my skills. Especially as I see he is a natural at watching the timing of my friend the green lady, and creating a beautiful, unspoken conversation with her as he darts slowly across her surface, turning the board as though they are reunited lovers on a dance floor.

It's magic to watch, really. I stand mesmerised for a little while. I watch the other wave warriors take up the dance with the green lady with full respect for her and her power – then working to see if they can meet her somewhere in the middle. An unspoken, unwritten song, when they are in tune it is beautiful and melodic, but if she switches the tempo, or they miss the timing of her rhythm… disaster, as they are ceremoniously dumped to recalibrate their egos, build that bravery back to its previous level and try again.

"Are you coming, or are you just going to stand there?"

I snap from my stare-bear state and grab my board. Nothing left to do now but strip down and get in the water. Except I still have my blue rashie from January. It just fits better now. So glad I changed my eating habits after the Grand Canyon.

I head in. Catch a little wave. Fall off. Rinse and repeat.

Laughter is a great way to get through these vulnerable moments. My skills are nowhere near his, but he is gracious in giving me some tips on timing and stance, and also laughing as I fall off.

"I'm going in – I need to check the time!"

He signals with a thumbs-up, following me back in to shore after the next wave.

As I grab my towel to dry off, he wraps his arms around me and kisses me.

"Hello!" he says.

"Um… hello."

"Well, this is nice."

I just grin like an idiot. "Sure is, but I have to get going. Mum duties beckon."

"Okay. I'm glad we got to do this. Was great."

"Sure was. So good for the soul."

"So good."

As we say our goodbyes, the awkwardness is not so awkward. Kind of nice. I leave feeling like I've caught a decent wave. That I am finally surfing this whole bravery thing. That maybe I have, before the year is out, nailed it. Yes, I'm awkward, but yes, I'm brave, and it is feeling like it is paying off.

11

NOVEMBER

*T*wo weeks later and I'm mid-pep talk with my dating guru slash relationship minefield sweeper, Jaq, who's already been-there-done-that and can safely pass the knowledge bombs onto me.

"Look at it this way, gorg: he did the right thing. It's like business. Think of online dating as covering different channels for business. You can go to networking events to meet people, or you can post online and do podcasts and Facebook Lives. Online dating is just another marketing channel to get yourself out there. Keep that beautiful heart of yours open and give it a go."

"You really think so?"

"One hundred percent. Just try a few different sites and see which one you like. Go on dates – it's just coffee – and see what you do and don't like. I'm really sorry that things didn't work out with Baker, but you know the saying…"

"What's right for him is right for me."

"Yep – that's the one. It will be okay, gorg. Don't be sad. Sometimes people are just in a different time and space. You were brave. It didn't work out, but at least you know, and now you can move on."

"I'd really like to get some closure, though, as I feel like I'm wondering what went wrong. I mean, maybe it is my body. Maybe it was all my stuff. Everyone has stuff at this age, though."

"And if that is who he really is, do you really want to be with someone like that?"

"No…"

Jaq. My beautiful friend who is the voice of reason. A five-foot-four pocket rocket with raven locks. If Anne Hathaway and Zooey Deschanel put their genetics together, and you popped them in the tumble dryer as though they were a cashmere jumper, and shrunk them a little, you'd have Jaq.

She's been through the whole dating thing. I have been her sideline partner and seen how brave she was in asking for what she wanted – which, for her, meant not wasting time and letting people know up-front that she was looking for the right person. She wanted to have a family, and she was prepared to do that with or without the right person, because, you know… biological clocks suck.

I did not have to ask for these things. I had the kids. I did, however, want to get back out there.

"Well, all you can do, really, gorg, is ask and see if he will have a chat with you."

"I wouldn't even know what to say."

"Stay on the higher ground. You don't want to make him feel bad, as you don't know what will happen in the future. Think about what you have learnt."

"Well, I guess I want to go out for dinner. I want to go on dates. I want to spend time getting to know someone – and have equal effort returned. I get logistics with kids and everything makes it hard, but for me, I guess my big lesson, like surfing, is that the alignment is in the action. You can't sit on the beach with a board and say you surf. You have to do the doing. I don't want to whinge about it. I want to get on with it."

"So what do you want to say?"

"Maybe… Maybe I need to thank him. He's helped me realise what I want, in a weird way, and he really has helped me to be brave."

"Okay. Well, just remember that he doesn't have to catch up with you. Some guys just won't do that. Remember what I said earlier. What's right for him is right for you, and you also never know what the future holds."

"I might have to sit and think about what to say first. I'd really like to understand what has happened."

"Well, start with that. Ask if he can help you learn what happened, as it might help you to grow as a person. And then you can thank him, as you have learnt through this process, gorg, as painful as it might feel."

Turns out that rejection – that wave – hurts. Being dumped sucks. But at least I know. I'd much rather ride the wave of knowing than sit on the beach of regret and never know. Good news, as painful as it is, is that my heart is open. It still works. I know I still feel. I know I haven't become super-hard because I've taken a risk and put myself out there.

At the end of October, I thought everything was going kind of okay. But radio silence happened after the big chat and kiss, and it threw me for six. Was it because he'd asked all these questions, and I'd been honest and told him the backstory?

No communication for nearly two weeks. Dating is such a weird space. I miss dating in my twenties, where it happened on a social level. Not everyone had a mobile phone. There was no social media, no Tinder, no Snapchat filter. No filter at all. The only filter was beer goggles. It happened the old-school way: at a Sunday session; at a pub, where people would actually talk to each other. They called, and if they didn't, sure, the angst was still there, but you moved on.

I decide, once again, to be brave and try to figure out what is going on. I send him a text. I mean, the least that can happen is a bit of courtesy.

Me: *Hey, just checking in that you are okay, and wondering if we can have a chat.*

Bakes: *Sure! Sounds serious. Should I be scared? Is this a face-to-face chat or a text chat?*

Me: *Well, I'd prefer a face-to-face chat, but if it has to be a text chat, then that is okay.*

Bakes: *Is everything okay?*

Me: *Um, no, not really. I could use your help to understand a couple of things, though.*

Bakes: *Okay. Same spot, about 3 pm?*

Me: *Sure. See you then.*

Summer is whispering that she is on her way. The days are longer, the air is warmer and the ocean is looking more like home. The only cool thing is Baker. But not the normal hot, happy cool.

He greets me with a hug, and then his body language switches. Arms fold across his chest. No more happy labrador. More serious-looking, dark and broody doberman. Out of character.

"Shall we just jump into this?" I start.

"As long as you are going to be nice about it. And I guess I owe you an explanation."

"Sooo… I'm guessing that there is something going on, and I just want to try to understand, as I'm finding the level of communication really odd, and I'm a fairly chatty person. I'll talk to my closest friends daily, and I'm trying to do the give-you-space thing and not be all weird, but getting back out there is weird and I haven't had to do this in a looong, long time so I have no idea what the rules are these days. So. Yeah."

My words spill out like verbal gastro. I can't stop vomiting them, like I ate a really bad prawn or something.

Once again, I watch his blue eyes look at me intently. I can see him processing what to say.

"I'm sorry. I really haven't done the right thing. I want to be able to take you out for dinner and hang out, but if I'm being really honest, I have to sort myself out with my job and my side business. You've made me realise that I can't stay where I am, work-wise, and I need to make a change, and really that means I'm not going to be able to give you the time that you need. It doesn't change how I feel about you as a person or anything. I still think you are inspiring and brave and amazing."

"Can you understand why I wanted to catch up? I just wasn't expecting you to ghost me. It seems out of character for you, and then, unfortunately, it brings up all these fears that I have been trying to get past. Like maybe it was my body. Maybe it's the fact that I have kids. Maybe I talk too much."

"Belle, no, it's not you. Your body is fine."

"Fine is a shit word. Fine is like un-hot."

"I like everything I see. I just am not being fair in trying to start something, as I don't know that I can offer you what you need. I mean, you have it together, and I don't. I need to sort it out."

"Well, I guess I've lost a good acupuncturist then."

The silence is sad. Maybe not sad. It's tinged with disappointment. Like the end of a movie where you thought there was going to be a different ending, and you walk out going, *Really? That kinda sucked.*

"Well… I do want to thank you, as you have made me realise I want someone who is prepared to be brave with me. I want to be taken out to dinner. I want to be seen. I want to go on adventures and have that person that is more like, 'Hey, let's figure it out.' Provided there is chemistry and neither of us are stalky and weird. So I guess I'll be venturing into the dating world after all."

He sits there staring out at the ocean.

"I'm just not in the same space as you right now, Belle. I mean, I might be in the future, but no one should have to put their lives on hold. I don't want you to do that. You might just be the one that gets away."

"Do you want a cracker to go with that cheesy line?"

"I mean it."

"I'm sorry – that's my defensive humour coming out. Just trying to make light of the situation. Just rejection sucks. Guess it's part of being brave. I'll be okay."

I lean over and kiss him on the cheek.

"Thanks, Bakes. I wish you all the happiness in the world, and hope you figure out your work and business stuff."

"So, can I call you and talk about it?"

"Nope. Same as I can't come see you for acupuncture. I can't be your coach. That's not what I am looking for. I'll just give myself a little time, and then get out there."

We say our goodbyes. As I drive to pick up my daughter, the rejection spills over and I'm feeling a bit Bridget Jones. I search through my playlist, finding Billie Eilish – my daughter's current favourite – and play 'When the Party's Over'.

Talk about waves. As I drive back to ballet college, there is pretty much a wave of rejection spilling out over my face.

I allow myself to feel, as painful as it is. I mean, this was the goal, right? To feel? To know I could be vulnerable? I'll get through this. I've gotten through worse things than rejection. Now, the tricky part will be to stay open, stay soft and not revert back to being shut down.

Time will sort things out. I won't even allow that much to pass. Distractions will work. Guess I'm going to have to be brave.

I park my car around the corner from Abby's ballet college and give myself time to just sit in it. As I walk towards her ballet college, something strange happens. I hear a little bit of a voice say, "Congratulations. You have learnt your last lesson. You are not meant to be hidden. You are worthy of living a brave and happy life. You can now have anything you want. Ask me for anything and you can have it."

Is this like my God moment? I mean, I have been saying 'the universe', but for me, the universe doesn't speak. It's a body of energy. And if it is God, it's been a long time between chats. Like, really long. But it's not a boomy voice or a calm voice. It's more of a fatherly, jokey voice. Like, if I were to think of the best coming-home, 'Hey, I'm so happy you are back' welcome and if God were to take the form of a dog, He'd probably be a beautiful golden retriever – watching and waiting for me through the window as I approach the door. It's a weird feeling. Like hearing from an old friend you have been out of touch with, but who you can hug it out with and be forgiven, and work to pick up where you left off.

Friday, the kids have a sports carnival. I hang back in the car park to call Becs before wandering over to watch everyone get a ribbon while they run, play tunnel ball, and do some other creative games that did not exist when I was a kid. Sports days are way more fun now.

"So, what happened? Jo told me about you catching up with Baker."

"I'm sorry I didn't say anything, I know you guys are friends, but anyway, it wasn't meant to be. Oooh! A bee just landed on my knee, Becs."

"Are you allergic?"

"No... it's just odd. He is just sitting on my knee. Anyway..."

"Bees are a good sign. They mean personal power and community, and they are lucky. This is a good sign, Belle."

"Oh, really? Well, this is odd. Because I have to tell you something, and it's going to feel weird. After the whole Baker thing didn't work out, something weird happened. And I get that you say 'the Universe', but I have to admit that when I think of the universe, I think of the stars and everything. I don't think of the universe as having a voice..."

"Okay, I'm waiting..."

"Well, don't think I'm weird or anything, because I think it is easier for people to accept woo these days than it is for people to accept spirituality and religious belief or something. But, um, it felt like God – not the universe – spoke."

I can hear the silence. Yep. Something I was hoping would not happen. Awkward, difference-of-spiritual-belief silence. Belle-is-turning-weird silence. Judgement silence.

"And what was it that was said?"

"Well. I kinda think it was like I could order a spiritual pizza. Like, if I ask for anything, and believe and value myself, that I can have anything I want. The message was: 'Congratulations, you have now learnt your last lesson. You can ask me for anything you want, and you can have it.'"

"Well that sounds like a pretty good voice. Best you order your pizza carefully, then."

"I will. I guess if it's 92 percent right, I'll say, thank you, but I asked for gluten free. Or something like that. I think there needs to be alignment."

"How? Like yoga?"

"No – alignment in definitions, and actions and words. They all have to line up."

⁓⁓⁓

Finally. I'm getting to meet Birdie. It's so nice to be sitting across from Jo at the Shorehouse. It's the last week of November and I've finished four coffee dates in the past week on the advice of Jaq. The sun is out, it's a kid-free weekend, and Jo and I get an in-real-life update. The place is bustling with the brunch crowd, and she's tag-teaming between me and her other friends before Birdie arrives.

"Did you see that table of men just turn and stare at you when you walked in? No, don't look. Oh my God it was funny. Man, you have lost weight. How much weight have you lost? You must be feeling really good. Don't lose any more."

Rapid-fire. I start laughing before I respond, "About 20 kilos, and yep – I'm feeling good. The whole wardrobe has had to get an update. Nothing fits. Should I look now? Where's Birdie?"

"No, don't look. She'll be here later, so we've got time for an update. So, tell me, what happened? I've been dying to know. What shall we call this one? Are you ho-bagging it?"

"I'd hardly call it ho-bagging. I've been on a couple of coffee dates... and yes, I broke the drought. Sort of... Maybe first-base drought. Well, maybe I should tell you what happened and what I've learnt."

"So, tell me. What's it like?"

"Well, I only lasted 48 hours on Tinder. It was like shark week. I felt like a bucket of chum. It's overwhelming."

"Why, what happened?"

"Well, my inbox blew up, I guess. Plus, as I have family sharing with the app store, I get a message from Abby saying, 'Mum, why have you got Tinder?' There was a good mum fail!"

"Hahaha, that's funny. What did you tell her?"

"Well, I had been out for drinks with one of the mums from the program. You remember Scarlett?"

"Yes! OMG I love her. How is she going?"

"Great. Anyway, we decided to download Tinder on my phone while having drinks for a bit of fun. After all, I'm still having a dry spell. My date life is going to be joining the farmers for drought relief."

Jo bursts out laughing to a snort-laugh level.

"Stop it. Do you want to know what it's like in heteroland after 40 with two kids?"

"Yeah, tell me, I'm dying to hear. Oooh, this means new code names. This will be fun." She claps her hands with excitement, and I watch her eyes light up.

"I think I might need to change my profile picture."

"Why is that?"

"I'm thinking I need to have a profile picture holding nuts and berries. Guys seem to like having pictures with fish, so I'm wondering if it's like a hunter-gatherer thing."

"Hahaha, maybe. Or maybe that is the only time they take pictures of themselves."

"I don't know. But anyway, I went on a few dates. Not ho-bagging. Just coffee."

"And what did you learn?"

"Well, guys have insecurities, too, and it's a frickin' minefield out there. I took my friend Jaq's advice and just decided to stay open and go and meet people and see what things were like. It means I'm testing my gut instinct to see if it's right or not."

"And? Is your gut right? Should you always listen to it?"

"Yes! OMG. Plus! There is this thing where I think you should ask a question about how old a picture is. I went out with a silver fox for coffee. Because I figure I'd allow a 10-year span – seven up, three down. So now it means I'm decade jumping.

"And...?"

"Well, couple of things. One you won't have to worry about if you decide to stay gay."

"Go on..."

"First date awkward for sure. Some of the people I've had coffee with are lovely, some are straight shooters. And then this silver fox, well, the date went down like this..."

"Do tell..."

I met a silver fox – let's call him Henry – at a café after a coaching client on a Friday. First impressions: much older than the profile pic. Like, by at least 10 years. Or there has been filtering and Snapchatting of photos. And no, he was not six foot one. He may have been pushing five foot eight. Which means when I pop on heels, which I was wearing, I'm taller. Like, a lot. I guess there are some truths people like to stretch.

The good thing I can say about chatting to a silver fox is they have the best stories. Intellectual. Smart. Smart to the point where I don't think they appreciate my dumb jokes and questions about, 'If you had to fight a shark or a crocodile, who would win?' I think they are done with that type of jokey banter. They could fake it, but it's just not their life zone.

I told the silver fox about how this year has been a project in bravery and trying new things, and that I kind of wanted to keep this outlook for life and be sure that I have adventures, as it's part of who I am.

This led the silver fox to sharing something that, well, was a bit of a wake-up call and also a bit of, *Oh my goodness I'm not ready for this. This is what getting older looks like.*

We were sitting in a little hip café in Fremantle. It was busy enough that our conversation didn't echo, and quiet enough so that we could hear the other person speaking. We had been talking about fitness and running and how there seem to be those who are into weight training, like me, and those diehard cardio fans, like him.

Silver fox segued, "So, I should let you know up-front that sometimes I experience, um, performance issues."

"What, like you can't run as fast as you used to? That's okay."

"No, I mean in the bedroom department."

"Oh, right. Um. And you are telling me this up-front because...?"

"Well, let's just say that some women can be cruel, and we all have issues as we get older, so my approach now is to tackle it front-on. I don't want to waste my time. I'm looking for my intellectual equal, and someone who appreciates the same things in life as me, and is kind."

"Are you happy to share? What happened, I mean? I can only guess that you might face body issues the same way that women do."

He stared at me, and composed himself.

"Well, this one woman referred to my penis as a dead mouse."

"Dead mouse? What?" My imagination starts going into overdrive as I can only start to visualise where this is headed.

"I hadn't told her about my performance issues. This was earlier on in my venture back into dating, and anyway, things had gotten hot and heavy as I had cooked her dinner, and it led to the bedroom."

"Oh, what did you cook?"

"Ragout. As she – you know – went downtown, I was not race ready, and she said, no word of a lie, 'Oooh, doesn't look very alive does it. Looks like a dead mouse! Let me be a kitty cat and see if I can bring it back to life.' So she started batting at my dick like she was a cat. It was humiliating. I've got a script for Viagra now. I don't like taking it all the time, though. It's not great."

I accidentally spat my coffee out. I couldn't help it. I was trying to stifle a laugh. I composed myself and tried to change topics.

"Oh, my. Well, that's new. I've never experienced that before. I've just learned to surf this year. I'm sorry, I didn't mean to react that way. You should know I'm a very visual person. And the whole cat-batting-dead-mouse thing, that is very visual."

The silver fox just stared at me. I think he willed my head to implode. So I tried to salvage the situation.

"Um, it's not the most important thing on my list, so thank you for being so brave and sharing. I imagine that would not be an easy topic to talk about."

"No. No, it's not. It's part of life, though. Do you think you'd like to catch up again?"

"Well, I'm really just getting out there, to be honest, so I'm going on coffee dates with a few people to see how it all works and goes down. It's a tough space, hey?"

"It's not easy. But I think you are whip-smart, and you are gorgeous, and you seem kind, so if you do want to catch up again, it would be lovely."

"Sounds like the silver fox is a bit of a gentleman," says Jo. "But do you really want to be dealing with those types of issues? Good to know he's open to fixing it, though."

"I'm just staying open for now. After the whole Hot Hands thing, I think I'll practise chatting to people. It's hard to find time to fit things in around business and kids' stuff, but I'm making space to meet someone. I believe we always make time for what's important. I think knowing life stages and similarities and differences is going to be important. I mean, he has grown kids. Mine are little. Intellectually it was great, but I do have to admit that he looks a little frail – like I might break him if I broke the drought – so no… won't be catching up with him again. I wouldn't rule out another silver fox, though."

"Okay, next? Let's give them code names." She claps her hands again with excitement.

"Well then there is the pastry chef. Interesting guy. Decided to learn to sing to be more vulnerable and put himself out there. I'd like to learn to sing properly. Thought he was kinda cool. But I think our definitions of health and fitness differ."

"In what area?"

"Well, I asked him what his drinking habits were like, considering he ordered three glasses of red."

"What time of day was this?"

"Lunch time."

"Oh, that seems a lot."

"He said he wasn't much of a drinker. So I asked him to define what that meant. His definition was maybe a bottle a night. Nothing excessive. You know, just a bottle of wine with dinner."

"Like a whole bottle?"

"A whole bottle."

"Well, that won't work. You hardly drink. At least you're learning what your boundaries are."

"Yes – I'm a bit shit with them sometimes, though."

"Ah, you can always change things. I mean, at the start of the year I wasn't a lesbian, but now I am. Hey, if you aren't having sex with any of these guys, you should go and get yourself a vibrator."

"Okay, okay, so you keep saying. I'm fine. Anyway, *oooh* – look whose eyes are lighting up!"

I watch my friend's face explode with high-school-girl-style giggles and joy.

A beautiful, short-haired, yoga-bodied soul appears next to Jo and kisses her on the cheek. Navy-blue shorts, loose-fitting white tee. A mop of brown curls, and a few sun-worn lines that tell me she probably loves the ocean and the earth. She seems like she has a warm, calming nature – the steadfast gumtree to Jo's whirly wind energy.

I stand up to greet her. "You must be Birdie."

"And you must be Belle – Jo has told me lots about you."

"But I don't want to have sex with her!" Jo bursts out.

It's funny, seeing my confident friend turn all awkward as she navigates her own bravery in being true to herself and exploring a new relationship dynamic. I chuckle.

We get the chance to chat to each other, and I watch two people very much in alignment re-tell the story of how they met, the twists life has taken, how they have both reconciled who they are, and the plans for overcoming any obstacles.

The "but I don't want to have sex with her!" line busts out at least three times, as Jo works to give Birdie assurance.

I start laughing. It's new ground for me, too.

"Birdie – just so you know, I don't want to have sex with Jo either. Actually, I don't want to have sex with either of you. Team peen over here. All the way. Nothing to worry about. So, tell me, what else have you got planned for today?"

Details unfold about going to catch up with old school friends, going for a walk around Fremantle, and normal things we do. The morning rolls on and Birdie ducks off to move her van to avoid a parking ticket, leaving Jo and I to wrap things up.

"Hey, Jo…"

"Yeah?"

"Thanks so much for being such a good friend. Do you know how rare it is to find someone you can be completely honest with and who will be there even if you fuck things up?"

"Yeah – we are pretty lucky that way. I love that we can say anything and that it's okay. Even if we don't like what the other person is saying or doing, it's nice to know that we are in each other's corner no matter what."

"Totally. Truth and honesty above all else. Thanks for being my fauxmily. Love you."

"Love you too. Hey – talk to you when I get home. Then you can update me on more dates. I'm really happy. I'm not fully out there yet, but I'm glad you know. I've still got to tell my family."

The dating foray continues, and life rolls on. Like surfing, it's all about finding the right conditions and timing. Being brave enough to make a dick of yourself and get back out there knowing that the right wave will turn up. No point sitting on the sidelines observing life.

As awkward and as weird as dating is, I'm beginning to think that the men are just as scared to get back out there.

Everyone has a bravery challenge. Everyone is brave in one way or another. Depends on how you want to live your life, really.

12

DECEMBER

*A*s I stand with my trusty, ginormous yellow foam surfboard in hand, I crunch my toes down into the sand, grounding my nerves. I'm still a shit surfer – just less shit now. I'm also 20 kilos lighter and feeling pretty good about life. I have a lot more joy. I am getting better at putting myself back out there. Both in the ocean and in the dating world.

It's the second surf for a Thursday. I've decided to have a bit of a chuck-it-in-the-fuck-it-bucket and go for a surf at Scarborough Beach while Abby is at Ballet College. There's a light easterly blowing.

Still a sea of dads. And some not-dads. I'd love to see some other mothers out here, though.

I look at the waves and think about where I will find a safe space to practise today. It's been a while since I've been to the beach and thought about safe spaces.

The last time I stood here, a safe space was created for me. A space where I could be awkward and vulnerable. I'm still awkward and vulnerable. I'm still fighting to not put up walls, to balance how much I give, and how much I allow myself to receive. I'm a work in progress, really.

I'm trying the online dating thing. It's weird. I'm learning that one person's definition of health may not be your definition of health. That one person's definition of 'I'm not much of a drinker' can mean one bottle of wine a night or one glass of wine a week. I'm trying to think about what I want when I'm a really old lady. I'm working out that, in some areas, I might actually be shallow. I do care about height. I do care about spirituality.

I know I want someone who is both my safe space and my greatest adventure. I know I don't want to be hidden – that if someone is going to be embarrassed about meeting you online, and concoct some story about meeting at a beginner lawn bowls meet, then that is on them, not on you. I don't do hidden anymore.

More than anything, though, I'm being brave. And I've learnt a few things this past year. Maybe I've even taught a couple of others a few things, too.

I've learnt that you are always going to hit a funk – even when you think you are funk-proof, one will just come and dunk you like a wave you missed your timing on. Maybe you take on something too big – you are out of your depth, you have thrown all regard for safety out the window, and are going gung-ho into the depths with no personal boundaries at all. You are testing your limits to see what you are made of. You are chasing down happiness, and at the same time, you are putting yourself at risk. Whichever one you focus on determines whether you move forward, or if you stay stuck in that place where unhappiness, unknowingness, resides.

Depending on the conditions, you'll either be tumbled through a pretty rough cycle, eventually pulling your head up, maybe a little disoriented, or maybe, if you are out of your depth, you will need to raise your hand and ask for help. And, surely enough, if you have your own lifesaver crew – like Becs, Jo, Lauren or Jaq – they will help get you back to shore to recover before encouraging you to get back out there again.

There is nothing greater in life than true friends. They are more than happy to watch you fall over, make mistakes, laugh with you – and at you, with love – cheer you on, cry, and really allow you to be 100 percent yourself. And they love you, and you love them. Just as you are. Not because you are family and it is an obligation or a duty, or something you feel you need to do to preserve the structure; but because you choose to, because you have your people. Your fauxmily.

I paddle out. I'm getting better at being out in the water. Some days I still feel like a fake. Like I shouldn't be here. Like I should be somewhere else. But I'd rather die chasing down my curiosity for life that is an embarrassment of riches, and a riches of embarrassments, because what I really know after that last big conversation with Baker is this:

Things are going to feel awkward. But awkward is where growth and learning lies. If we are truly lucky, we are given a safe space to be brave. One where that awkwardness is seen for its intent and its action.

Because at the end of the day, the outcome for all of us is the same. The outcome doesn't really matter – the process and actions along the way are what matter. How we treat ourselves, and how we treat each other. How we forgive others and ourselves for our mistakes, and try to understand why they happened in the first place. How we are never really ready; some waves we will see coming, and some catch us completely by surprise.

And maybe, like today, the conditions are favourable. Maybe you have a really good run, catch a few waves and are feeling awesome. Then, for whatever reason, things change. The wind changes, you place a foot wrong, you miss your mark.

Disappointment sets in. I try one more time and get pummelled. Again. I'm starting to hurt and know it's time to take a break. Time for recovery before I go out again. I head back to shore, dragging big yellow along with me, saying hi to faces that are starting to become familiar.

Then I hear a voice from behind.

"Ahem. Are you planning on putting that back?"

I turn around and look up, to be greeted by a smile. A hand reaches forward and grabs the huge wad of seaweed caught in my wetsuit zipper like some bad mermaid mullet. He hands it to me like a weird bunch of flowers. *Typical, Belle, typical.*

"That was quite a wave."

"Yes, yes it was."

EPILOGUE

"*M*um, it's okay. Do you know what you are really good at?" Abby says.

"Catching waves? Singing in the car?"

"You are really good at trying new things, and not giving up when things get hard."

"Aw, chicken. I love you. Thanks for seeing me."

And so I taught her how to be brave.